Kartar S writer. He stories, ten more than fit plays, an autobiography and several works of literary criticism. He has been honoured with the Padma Bhushan, the Soviet Land Nehru Award and Punjab Sahitya Akademi's Sarva-Saresht Sahityakar Award for the totality of his contribution to Indian literature besides the National Academy of Letters Award for short stories, the Ghalib Award for Drama, the Bhasha Parishad Award for fiction and the Bhai Mohan Singh Award for autobiography. In recognition of his contribution to Indian literature, Duggal was conferred the degree of D.Litt (*Honoris Causa*) by the Punjabi University in 1994. Having served as Director, All India Radio, Director, National Book Trust, and Adviser (Information) in the Planning Commission of India, he is currently devoted exclusively to literary activity.

Other titles by the Author
in UBSPD

The Akal Takht
and Other Seats of Sikh Polity

The Sikh People : Yesterday and Today

The Sikh Gurus : Their Lives and Teachings

Orphans of the Storm : Stories on the Partition of India
(co-editor)

Select Sikh Scriptures – 1
Guru Nanak

Compiled and Transcreated
by
K.S. Duggal

UBSPD

UBS Publishers' Distributors Ltd.
New Delhi ● Mumbai ● Bangalore ● Madras
Calcutta ● Patna ● Kanpur ● London

UBS Publishers' Distributors Ltd.

5 Ansari Road, New Delhi-110 002
Phones : 3273601, 3266646 ✶ *Cable* : ALLBOOKS ✶ *Fax* : (91) 11-327-6593
e-mail: ubspd.del@smy.sprintrpg.ems.vsnl.net.in
Apeejay Chambers, 5 Wallace Street, Mumbai-400 001
Phones : 2046971, 2047700 ✶ *Cable* : UBSIPUB ✶ *Fax* : 2040827
10 First Main Road, Gandhi Nagar, Bangalore-560 009
Phones : 2263901, 2263902, 2253903 ✶ *Cable* : ALLBOOKS ✶ *Fax* : 2263904
6, Sivaganga Road, Nungambakkam, Chennai-600 034
Phone : 8276355 ✶ *Cable* : UBSIPUB ✶ *Fax* : 8270189
8/1-B, Chowringhee Lane, Calcutta-700 016
Phones : 2441821, 2442910, 2449473 ✶ *Cable* : UBSIPUBS ✶ *Fax* : 2450027
5 A, Rajendra Nagar, Patna-800 016
Phones : 652856, 653973, 656170 ✶ *Cable* : UBSPUB ✶ *Fax* . 656169
80, Noronha Road, Cantonment, Kanpur-208 004
Phones : 369124, 362665, 357488 ✶ *Fax* : 315122

© K.S. Duggal

First Published **1997**

K S Duggal asserts the moral right to be identified as the author of this work.

37386340

Cover Design: Ilaksha

Designed & Typeset at UBSPD in 12 pt. Times Roman
Printed at Rajkamal Electric Press, New Delhi

For
My children
Shehla and Suhel

Contents

Introduction

As it descends, the Lord's Word,
I deliver it, O Lalo!

TILANG (722)

Thus confided Guru Nanak in Bhai Lalo, one of his
earliest followers. Author of more than 900 hymns (as
recorded in the Holy Graṇth), Guru Nanak was no
ordinary poet. He was a messenger of God, albeit an
otherwise utterly humble soul, who described himself as
the dust of the feet of even minions, Guru Nanak took
considerable pride in professing to be a poet. More than
once he says:

He does and makes you do as He desires
So says Nanak, the poet.

ASA (434)

Essentially the ecstatic pourings of a spiritual seeker,
Guru Nanak's hymns are a significant step in the
scriptural lore of the subcontinent.

Guru Nanak was born and brought up in *bar* (the
upland between two river valleys in the Punjab plains)

1

where he had to weather severe summers and dreary winters. The rainy season was, however, enchanting and so was the spring. The region had rich crop-laden fields and thick jungles, with a variety of birds and beasts. Guru Nanak absorbed completely his milieu, the well-knit, Elysian rural setting, in which the headman of the village was a God-fearing Muslim and his revenue record-keeper a Hindu. He makes several references to his environments:

> *With the spring and the pretty bumble-bee,*
> *The plants in the orchards are in bloom.*

> *The clouds have gathered low,*
> *They pour as they please.*

> *The grasshoppers wail in the forest,*
> *The lightning flashes and frightens.*

> *There is water in pools and plains;*
> *The rainy season is for rejoicing.*
> *It rains during the dark night,*
> *How can the young bride be at peace?*

> *The frogs and peacocks cry aloud,*
> *The pied cuckoo calls to her sweetheart.*

BARAH MAH (1107-10)

Guru Nanak described his times in a most telling manner;

> *Kaliyuga is a dagger,*
> *Kings are butchers.*
> *Dharma has taken wings and flown away;*
> *In the black night of falsehood*
> *The moon of truth is nowhere to be seen.*
> *I am lost in the search,*
> *I find no way out of darkness.*
> *Afflicted with ego, I wail in sorrow,*
> *Says Nanak, how do I attain deliverance?*
>
> RAGA MAJH (145)

Guru Nanak condemned the corrupt ways of the administration as vehemently:

> *There is none*
> *who receives or gives not bribe*
> *Even the king distributes justice*
> *When his palm is greased.*

It was, indeed, the worst of times. It is said that when evil exceeds all limits, God takes pity on His creation and sends a Messiah to show light to the people. Thus was born Guru Nanak.

Unlike Mahavira and Buddha, Nanak was not born to affluent parents. He was the son of Mehta Kalian Das, a village patwari, at the lowest rung of the revenue hierarchy. Mehta Kalian Das led a clean life; he was honest and God-fearing, rare qualities in those days. He was, therefore, greatly respected by the Muslim headman of the village, Rai Bular.

Born on 15 April 1469 at Talwandi in Sheikhupura district in West Punjab, Nanak was the only son of his parents. Their other child was a daughter called Nanaki, born a few years earlier. The son arrived after a long wait. His mother, Tripta, and his sister, Nanaki, doted on him. His father, however, was too involved with work to spare any time to be with his children.

Mehta Kalian Das, also known as Mehta Kalu, was a Bedi, a caste supposed to be well-versed in the Vedas. As a child, Nanak was given the name Nanak Rai in the tradition of the Hindus of the day. Talwandi, the village where he was born, came to be known, in due course, as Nanakana Sahib — the holy city of Nanak. It is located about 50 km to the north-west of Lahore, the capital of the West Punjab, in Pakistan.

While playing with other children, Nanak was always fair. He made friends with the poor and the so-called low-castes. The Hindu and Muslim boys were equally good friends of his. He had a melodious voice and liked to sing devotional songs. When he sang he went into a trance, as it were; phrases tripped on his lips and he composed hymns extempore. He would take long walks and go out of his village into the fields and jungles, both in the morning and in the evening. There was always a freshness on his face, a soothing light in his eyes. He was genial and gentle, suave, soft-spoken and sweet-tempered.

Nanak's sister, Nanaki, was deeply attached to him. She wondered whether it was because he was her only brother, but she knew it was more than that. Every time she saw Nanak, she felt a tug at her heart; he was indeed unlike other children. When he was asleep, Nanaki saw a strange glow on his face. It was enchanting to watch him. She would look at him for hours on end. Sitting alone sometimes, she would suddenly sense a sweet fragrance spreading around the courtyard and turning her face she would find her younger brother enter the house, arm-in-arm with one of his playmates. When he sat in the prayer chamber, she would hear the beating of cymbals and *arati* being sung in praise of God. She would remain glued to where she sat. It was as if divine music were descending from heaven; the melody was exquisite. No doubt her brother was no ordinary child. But she dared not talk about it to anyone; it was a closely-guarded secret.

Nanak, who was to emerge in due course as the Divine Master, had his first devotee in his own sister. She found in her brother an evolved soul, a messenger of God.

The second disciple of Nanak was Rai Bular, the Muslim chief of the village. Day after day, week after week, month after month and year after year, he heard amazing stories about Mehta Kalu's child. His utterances astonished both the Hindus and the Muslims _ they found them bold and meaningful and endowed with an unusual charm.

The village schoolteacher Gopal Panda soon found that there was little left he could teach Nanak. Nanak learnt reading and writing very quickly. He even composed an acrostic on the Punjabi alphabet which was perhaps also the first hymn he composed. When the teacher tried to teach him arithmetic, he found Nanak proficient in figure work too. Nanak told his teacher that without knowledge of God all knowledge is meaningless. Without truth, even a cartload of books is of little use:

> *Burn worldly love,*
> *Grinding it into ashes to make ink.*
> *Let your intellect be the fine paper*
> *On which you write*
> *With the pen of divine love,*
> *As dictated by the Guru.*
> *Write the praises of His Name*
> *Write that he is Limitless and Great.*
> *Oh teacher, if you were to learn writing this*
> *The truth of it will stand by you*
> *Wherever you are called upon to render account.*

SRI RAGA (16)

Nanak was then sent to a *madrasa* (a place where higher learning is imparted) to learn Persian and Arabic. His teacher was Ruknuddin. The understanding was that after he acquired proficiency in Persian, he might, in due course, succeed his father as the village *patwari*. Rai Bular would be very happy to have him work with him. Nanak surprised his new teacher also by picking up Persian and Arabic quickly. One day he astonished Ruknuddin with an acrostic composed on the Perso-Arabic alphabets.

In due course, Nanak was to be invested with the sacred thread, the *janeau*, according to a custom prevalent among the caste Hindus. It is akin to the sacrament-like baptism amongst Christians, signifying the spiritual rebirth of the Hindu child. Hardyal, the family priest, was invited to perform the ritual in the presence of relatives, friends and neighbours. The ceremony was to be followed by a lavish feast and rejoicing. However, when the presiding priest approached Nanak to invest him with the sacred thread, Nanak declined to wear it; young Nanak had no faith in the ritual, and would have nothing to do with the thread which would sooner or later wear out.

Everyone present was stunned. They tried to argue with the child, but none succeeded in persuading him. When the priest persisted, Nanak went into a trance and sang:

> *Let mercy be the cotton, contentment the thread,*
> *Continence the knot, and truth the twist.*
> *O priest! If you have a sacred thread of the like*
> *Do give it to me.*
> *It won't wear out or get soiled,*
> *Neither burn nor get lost.*
> *Says Nanak, blessed are those who go about*
> *wearing such a thread.*

RAGA ASA (471)

Rai Bular who had been invited to participate in the feast following the thread ceremony was thrilled to hear the verse. He complimented Mehta Kalu on his son's talents. But Mehta Kalu, a devout Hindu, was heart-broken.

As he grew, Nanak spent more and more time in the company of Hindu anchorites and Muslim dervishes, in the thick forest around Talwandi; he was happiest in their company. But the matter-of-fact Mehta Kalu did not approve of it. "If he is fond of wandering about in the forest," he said to himself, "he might as well take the cattle out to graze. He could spend his time in the fields as well as look after the cattle." Nanak agreed. He liked grazing cows and buffaloes. Accordingly, he led his cattle out to graze every morning and brought them back in the evening when it was time to milk them. Before long, the flock was completely tamed. It didn't bother the cowherd at all. As Nanak sat under the trees and sang hymns, the cattle grazed on and frolicked about.

Then, one day, an agitated peasant came and complained to Rai Bular that Mehta Kalu's cattle had ravaged his entire crop and that his son sent to look after the cattle was found sleeping under a tree. Rai Bular, who understood Nanak better, didn't believe a word. He decided to verify the loss himself. Out in the field, he did find Nanak sitting under a tree, lost in deep meditation but the crop alleged to have been ravaged by the cattle was intact, not a blade seemed to have been disturbed. The peasant who had lodged the complaint could not believe his eyes. He felt frightfully embarrassed. Rai Bular, then, walked up to the tree where Nanak sat. He found that there was a halo around his head. He was convinced that Mehta Kalu's son was a blessed soul, and he bowed to him in reverence.

Rai Bular made indulgent inquiries about Nanak — where he spent his time, what he did and so on. Even if it meant going out of the way, he would drop in at Mehta Kalu's house and meet Nanak. Every time Rai Bular looked at Nanak, he was charmed. His head would bow before him spontaneously. Every word that Nanak uttered acquired new significance; it haunted him day and night.

Mehta Kalu, on the other hand, did not understand a word of what his son said. In fact, he was irritated at the fuss his daughter Nanaki and his mentor Rai Bular made over his son. He thought Nanak was good-for-nothing; the only son, he was being pampered by his people and was getting spoilt. Mehta Kalu also thought that Nanak showed little interest in any worthwhile activity, and that of late he had developed a strange tendency to keep to himself; as far as possible, he avoided company, and remained lost in thought. His eyes were dreamy. He didn't eat for days together. At night, when everybody slept, Mehta Kalu often saw his young son deeply absorbed in meditation. At times he thought he heard his sobs, and at others, he saw tears rolling down Nanak's cheeks. It wrenched his heart.

Everyone who saw Nanak during those days felt that there was something wrong with him. He appeared to be suffering from some ailment. It was, therefore, decided to have the youth examined by a *vaid*.

Hari Das, a leading physician, was sent for. As the old physician was feeling his pulse, Nanak went into a

trance and started reciting a hymn. The physician, spell-
bound, listened to his patient:

> *The physician has been sent for*
> *To prescribe a remedy;*
> *He pulls my arm*
> *And feels the pulse.*
> *A simpleton, the physician knows not*
> *The ache is deep in the chest.*

RAGA MALAR (1276)

> *I suffer pangs of separation*
> *I hunger for Him and suffer,*
> *I suffer the fear of dreadful death,*
> *I suffer from the ills*
> *That must have me as their kill.*
> *And no remedy of the* vaid *would help.*
> *It's an eternal agony,*
> *No remedy of the* vaid *would help*
> *However potent.*
> *I forgot God, indulged in pleasure-giving*
> *pursuits.*
> *And thus I contracted many an ailment.*
> *I went blind; I must be punished,*
> *And no remedy of the* vaid *would help.*

RAGA MALAR (1256)

The physician heard Nanak and his eyes opened:
Nanak certainly suffered from a malady whose cure was
beyond his remedy.

The anxious parents decided to get their son married before it was too late. They thought that, bound in marriage, Nanak might begin to take interest in household affairs he might even take to some profitable pursuit. Accordingly, a suitable match was found in Sulakhni, the daughter of Mula, a Chona Khatri. Mula was also a *patwari* at Pakho di Randhawa (now in Pakistan). Nanak did not object to it; he maintained that married life was not in conflict with spiritual pursuits, if anything, it only helped.

Nanak was happily married. He loved his wife. They had two sons — Sri Chand was followed three years later by Lakshmi Chand. Now that he had a family of his own, Nanak was persuaded by his father to engage himself in some profitable pursuit, so that in due course he could be on his own. The father's counsel was, indeed, reasonable, and Nanak readily agreed to it. Mehta Kalu was most happy at this development. He lost no time in placing a suitable sum at his disposal and deputed Bala, one of his menials, to assist Nana! It was decided that they go to Chuhrkana, a wholesale market (in the present-day Gujranwala district of Pakistan) to make a profitable bargain.

Nanak did go to Chuhrkana. He did make the purchases that could make a profit back home. But during his return journey, he encountered a band of holy men, who, it seemed, had had nothing much to eat for several days. They didn't have any clothes either and winter was fast approaching. Nanak saw their plight and didn't take a moment to decide to feed and clothe them with what he carried.

Placing all his purchases at the disposal of the holy men, Nanak, along with Bala, walked back home empty-handed. As he came close to his village, he suddenly realized how his father would react to the peculiar bargain he had struck. Instead of going home, he sat under a tree outside the village.

When his father learnt this, he was livid. Nanak tried to explain to him that he had been sent to make a profitable bargain and that he could not think of a better deal. Mehta Kalu didn't understand. As it happened, Rai Bular also turned up on the scene and, listening to Nanak arguing with his father, he was convinced that Nanak was indeed no ordinary youth. Rai Bular became Nanak's devoted disciple.

But Mehta Kalu continued to feel miserable. He was troubled by the ways of his son. Neither Rai Bular nor his daughter could make him see the divine in Nanak. The tree under which Nanak sat outside the village, fearing the wrath of his father, still exists. It is known as Thamb Saheb – the holy trunk. The devout meditate under it.

Nanak's sister Nanaki had been married to Jai Ram, a Khatri, employed as a steward by Daulat Khan Lodi, the Governor of Sultanpur. Jai Ram, visiting Talwandi and finding his father-in-law anxious about his son, offered to take Nanak along with him to Sultanpur and find a job for him with his master. Everyone approved. Nanak, too, didn't object. Rai Bular wrote to Daulat Khan recommending Nanak in glorious terms.

Daulat Khan met Nanak and was most favourably impressed by the charm of his personality and the transparent honesty of his character. He asked Nanak to take charge of his stores. It was the most appropriate assignment for a God-fearing man like Nanak. A few days later, Mardana, one of Nanak's companions at Talwandi, also joined him. Mardana was an instrumentalist by profession; he played the *rabab*.

During the day Nanak worked in the Nawab's commissariat; in the mornings and evenings Nanak and Mardana would get together to meditate and sing hymns. Their sessions became longer and longer. More and more people joined them.

Before he left his home in Talwandi, Nanak had promised his wife that he would send her a part of his earnings which he did. With the rest of his money he entertained his companions, and the poor and the needy that he came across. It is said that Nanak remained in the service of the Nawab for about two years.

Early one morning, Nanak, accompanied by Mardana, went to a nearby stream called Bain for his bath. This was the first thing he did every day. To Mardana's surprise, after Nanak plunged into the water that morning, he didn't reappear on the surface. Mardana waited and waited. Then, panic-stricken, he ran to the town to seek assistance. Evidently, Nanak had either been drowned or was washed away by the stream that was in spate. The Nawab, who by now had become a great admirer of Nanak, got the best divers to scrounge the bed of the stream thoroughly. But Nanak was nowhere to be found.

Then some wicked people started a whispering campaign. They alleged that Jai Ram's brother-in-law had embezzled the stores and, fearing the consequences, had fled or may have committed suicide by drowning himself. The stores were thoroughly checked and it was found that the inventory and the accounts were absolutely in order.

To everybody's delight, Nanak appeared in the town after three days as if from nowhere. There was great relief in the Nawab's household and rejoicing among Nanak's relatives and friends. But Nanak was not his old self; he was a changed man. There was divine light in his eyes and his face was resplendent. A halo seemed to surround his head. People flocked to have a glimpse of him.

Nanak wouldn't speak to anybody. He was in a trance. He gave up his job with the Nawab and distributed all that he had to the poor. Accompanied by Mardana, the *rabab* player, he left the town.

When he broke his silence after a few days, his first utterance was: "There is no Hindu, there is no Mussalman." He spoke in ecstasy. He was no more Nanak, the dreamy-eyed youth from Talwandi; he was Guru Nanak, a messenger of God, ordained to propagate His Name and the virtues of truthfulness and clean living.

His second utterance was: "One must labour to earn and share one's earnings with others." When he started his life-long mission, these were the two cardinal principles of Guru Nanak's teachings. It is said that he was thirty years old when he left Sultanpur.

Before Nanak took his leave the Nawab asked Guru Nanak what he had meant when he said — "There is no

Hindu, there is no Mussalman". The Nawab said that Hindus may not be Hindus but the Mussalmans remained devoted to their faith. By way of explanation Guru Nanak uttered these words:

Let compassion be your mosque,
Devotion your prayer-mat,
Truth and fair play the Holy Qur'an,
Let your modesty be your circumcision
And courtesy the fast of a Muslim.
Your conduct be the Kaaba,
Rectitude your guide,
And good deeds your creed and prayer.
The rosary should be what pleases Him.
Thus would He safeguard your honour.

RAGA MAJH SLOK (140)

The *qazi* in the Nawab's court, however, was not convinced. "If you are not a Hindu," he said, "you must join us in prayers, we are devout Muslims, who believe in the unity of God." Guru Nanak was certainly willing to keep company with those who had faith in God. He agreed to join them in prayers. But when the *qazi* commenced the prayers, Guru Nanak stood aside and watched with a smile on his lips. As soon as the prayers were over, the infuriated *qazi* asked Guru Nanak, "Why didn't you join us in prayers after agreeing to do so?" Guru Nanak told him politely, "I did not join you because all the while you were saying your prayers, your mind was on your filly which was left loose at your home. You feared that she might drop into the well of your courtyard." The *qazi* heard Guru Nanak and was silenced. "In that case, you could have given me your company," said the Nawab. "Yes, but you were buying horses at Kabul," observed Guru Nanak. Hearing this, the Nawab fell at the Guru's feet. Guru Nanak was, indeed, a man of God. God spoke through him.

Leaving Sultanpur, Guru Nanak came to Saidpur, a small town later known as Eminabad (in Gujranwala district of Pakistan). Guru Nanak chose to stay here with Lalo, a carpenter.

The day Guru Nanak arrived, the chief of the town, Malik Bhago, who had amassed untold wealth, was holding a sacrificial feast to which all the holy men were invited. Guru Nanak decided to remain away and partook of the simple fare of his host. When Malik Bhago came to know of this, he was furious. "How dare an itinerant mendicant refuse my invitation?" he asked, in vulgar pride. He had Guru Nanak brought to him. When asked why he didn't join in the sacrificial feast which every other holy man in the town had blessed with his presence, the Guru sent for the meal served by Malik Bhago and also Bhai Lalo's simple fare. It is said when Guru Nanak holding a part of each in separate hands squeezed, to the utter discomfiture of Malik Bhago, what appeared like blood dropped from his rich food, and milk seemed to ooze out of Bhai Lalo's simple fare. Malik Bhago was put to shame; he didn't have to be told that his riches were amassed by exploiting the poor, while what Bhai Lalo offered was the milk of hard-earned wages. Malik Bhago became a changed man. He distributed all his ill-gotten wealth to the poor and needy and devoted himself to the service of his fellowmen.

Bhai Lalo craved Guru Nanak's company longer but the Guru had to proceed on his mission. After several days of journeying through jungles and wilderness, Guru Nanak, accompanied by Mardana, arrived at a caravanserai which was maintained by a saintly-looking man called Sajjan. The caravanserai had tidy rooms for travellers, and both a mosque and a temple for their prayers.

All this was, however, a cover for Sajjan's misdeeds. He was, in fact, a robber and an assassin. He would loot travellers who came to stay with him and, if need be, have them killed. Sajjan usually attacked his victims during the night when they were asleep. Noticing the glow on Guru Nanak's face, Sajjan mistook him for a prosperous trader who he thought was, perhaps, travelling in the guise of a recluse to avoid being waylaid. He waited and waited that night but Guru Nanak would not retire. Late in the night, when everyone else had gone to sleep, Guru Nanak sang, Mardana accompanying him on the *rabab*:

> *Bright and brilliant is the bronze,*
> *But the moment it is rubbed its blackness*
>   *appears;*
> *This cannot be removed even if washed a*
>   *hundred times.*

SUHI (729)

Guru Nanak sang this hymn, evidently directed at Sajjan who was, all this while, waiting for an opportunity to pounce upon his visitor. Guru Nanak's words touched him at the core of his heart. He realized his folly. He came out of his hiding place and fell at the Guru's feet, confessing all his misdeeds. The den of the assassin was transformed into a *dharmasala*, seat of Dharma. It was the first major centre that Guru Nanak set up for the congregation of his disciples.

During his sojourn towards the east, Guru Nanak camped in a small town. The rains came and he had to stay in the town longer than he had thought he would. Several devotees came to the Guru regularly. Amongst them were two close friends who lived in the same lane. On their way to see the Guru, one of them came across a courtesan and was allured by her charm. Thereafter, he left his home along with his friend on the pretext of going to the Guru but instead visited his paramour. A few days later the one who came to pay his homage to the Guru daily was pricked with a thorn, while his neighbour who visited the prostitute found a gold coin in the street. The incident bewildered the Guru's devotee who came to him every day religiously. He mentioned it in the prayer meeting that morning. Guru Nanak heard it and was amused. He then told the Sikh:

Your friend was destined to come across a treasure but because of his evil ways, the treasure was reduced to a single coin. On account of your past Karma you were to be

impaled with a stake but because you reformed
yourself, you have been let off with the mere
prick of a thorn.

When the rains abated, Guru Nanak, accompanied by
Mardana, came to Kurukshetra (in today's Ambala
district in Haryana) where a big fair was being held at
the holy tank on account of the solar eclipse. A large
number of pilgrims from all over the country had
gathered there. When they arrived at the fair, Guru
Nanak asked Mardana to cook meat for them. As it
happened, they had been presented deer meat by a
shikari while on their way to Kurukshetra. Finding a
pilgrim cooking meat on the holy premises, the Yogis
collected for the fair were scandalized. How could
anyone defile the sacred premises with the profanity of
cooking and eating meat? They gathered around Guru
Nanak and started shouting at him. Guru Nanak heard
them patiently and then sang thus:

> *Implanted by flesh, conceived in flesh,*
> *You nested in flesh.*
> *When infused with life*
> *Your mouth, bones, skin and body were created*
> *in flesh,*
> *Emerging out of the flesh (of the womb),*
> *You had breasts of flesh to suck.*
> *Your mouth is of flesh; of flesh is your tongue,*
> *It is with flesh that you breathe.*
> *As you grow, you wed*
> *And bring home flesh.*
> *Flesh gives birth to flesh.*

All your relatives have ties of flesh.
It is when one meets the True Guru
That things get sorted out.
There is no emancipation on one's own.
Says Nanak, mere talking leads to nothing.

MALAR (1289)

The pilgrims collected around Guru Nanak heard him and were silenced. The Guru told them to meditate on God alone and address one another with the salutation *Sat Kartar* (God is Truth) and he went his way.

Guru Nanak's next halt was at Hardwar, a Hindu centre of pilgrimage on the banks of the holy Ganges. Here the Guru found a large gathering of devotees bathing in the river and offering water to the sun.

"Why do you throw water like that?" Guru Nanak asked a pilgrim.

"It is to propitiate our ancestors," the latter replied.

Guru Nanak heard him and, turning the other way, began throwing water towards the west.

"What are you doing?" asked a fellow pilgrim. "The sun at this hour is in the east, not in the west."

"I am not offering water to the sun. I am trying to water my lands in a village near Lahore," said Guru Nanak.

"But my good man, how will the water reach your crops so far away?"

"If your water can reach your ancestors in the region of the sun, why can't mine reach my fields a short distance from here?" asked Guru Nanak.

He had a subtle sense of humour and could at times make his point effortlessly.

Guru Nanak passed through Panipat, where he met a successor of Shaikh Sharaf, a disciple of Khwaja Qutbuddin, and then proceeded to Delhi, where he refused to work a miracle at the instance of Ibrahim Lodi, the ruling monarch of the time. Later Guru Nanak went to Brindaban where he witnessed a performance of Ras Lila and rejected it as a sheer waste of breath and devoid of the spirit of devotion. While journeying towards the east, Guru Nanak is said to have visited Gorakhmata, a temple devoted to Gorakh Nath, situated not far from Pilibhit. Here, it is believed, the soapnut tree under which Guru Nanak camped suddenly wore a verdant look. It attracted many an ascetic residing at the centre to come and discourse with the Guru. Guru Nanak told them what real asceticism is:

> *Asceticism doesn't lie in ascetic robes; nor in*
> *the walking staff, nor in the ashes,*
> *Asceticism doesn't lie in the earring, the shaven*
> *head, or in blowing a conch;*
> *Asceticism lies in remaining pure amidst impurities.*
> *Asceticism doesn't lie in mere words,*
> *He an ascetic is who treats everyone alike,*
> *Asceticism doesn't lie in visiting burial and*
> *cremation grounds.*
> *It lies not in wandering about, nor in bathing*
> *at places of pilgrimage;*
> *Asceticism lies in remaining pure amidst impurities.*
> *On meeting with the True Guru doubts are dispelled*
> *and the restlessness of the mind stilled,*

*It drizzles nectar, a steady melody is heard and
    there is enlightenment within;
Asceticism lies in remaining pure amidst impurities.
Says Nanak, asceticism lies in death in life,
The conch sounds without being blown
And there is a feeling of fearlessness;
Asceticism lies in remaining pure amidst
impurities.*

SUHI (730)

The ascetics were greatly moved at Guru Nanak's
utterances; Gorakhmata came to be known as Nanakmata
and is a place of pilgrimage even today.

While passing through Bihar, Guru Nanak is said to
have visited Gaya, where Gautam Buddha attained
enlightenment.

Guru Nanak, accompanied by Mardana, then went to
Assam. In Kamrup he encountered Nur Shah who
practised black magic. Nur Shah heard about the Guru's
arrival and sent her scouts to ensnare him with their
wiles. They succeeded with Mardana who happened to
have gone to the town in search of food. They charmed
and made a lamb of him; with their hypnotic power,
they made him bleat and behave like a lamb.

Guru Nanak was aware of this and was greatly
amused. After a while, he went to the rescue of his
disciple. The wicked women tried their wiles on Guru
Nanak too. Her companions having .failed Nur Shah
herself tried to bewitch Guru Nanak with her charms.
Nur Shah, who had vanquished many an ascetic in her
life, was bewildered at Guru Nanak's spiritual prowess.

Having tried all her spells and failed, she accepted defeat and fell at the Guru's feet.

It was again during this journey that Mardana fell into the clutches of Kauda, a head-hunter. It is said that everytime Kauda tried to kindle the fuel in the oven so that he could roast Mardana, it would not catch fire. He tried again and again until Guru Nanak appeared on the scene and showed light to the cannibal.

On his way back from Assam, Guru Nanak returned via Orissa visiting the famous temple of Lord Jagannath at Puri. This temple is one of the most important places of Hindu pilgrimage. Guru Nanak found that the priests attached more importance to rituals than to true faith in God. They would make elaborate arrangements to propitiate the deity, with trays full of burning candles, flowers and all sorts of perfumes, both in the mornings and in the evenings. They called it *arati*; Guru Nanak found that none of the devotees joining the ritual had his heart in it. At best, people enjoyed the spectacle of it. He left the congregation, went out of the temple and, sitting in a corner, started singing his own *arati*, an ode to God, with Mardana accompanying him on the *rabab*.

> *The sky is the platter,*
> *The Sun and the Moon are the lights,*
> *And stars the jewels,*
> *Sandalwoods' fragrance is the incense,*
> *The wind is the flywhisk,*
> *And all the forests Your flowers.*
> *What a wonderful arati it is!*
> *Oh, You destroyer of life and death!*

It's an unending strain — the melody of
Your Name.
You have a thousand eyes and yet not one eye.
You have a thousand forms and yet not one form.
You have a thousand unsoiled feet and yet not
one unsoiled foot.
You have a thousand noses and yet not one nose.
Your ways have left me charmed, Oh Lord!
There is my Lord's light which enlightens
everyone.
By the Guru's grace the truth becomes manifest.
The arati is what pleases God.
I hunger for the fragrance of your lotus feet day
and night.
Oh Lord! Grant a drop of water of Your grace,
To Nanak, the thirsty bird,
So that he finds solace in your Name.

DHANASRI (633)

In the meanwhile, the priests and pilgrims had collected around Guru Nanak and they were thrilled to hear him sing the praises of God. His melody seemed to touch their hearts. They were delighted to have such an enlightened soul amongst them. They remembered Guru Nanak for long after he left them.

Guru Nanak returned home after a little over twelve years, more because Mardana had begun to miss his family. He wished to visit his family and provide for them before he accompanied Guru Nanak on his proposed journey to the south. Guru Nanak chose to stay back in the forest and asked Mardana to return after he had attended to his filial obligations. However, when Guru Nanak's parents heard about Mardana's return, Mata Tripta knew that her son could not be far. Though Mardana, as advised by Guru Nanak, did not reveal to them his whereabouts, they traced Guru Nanak to the forest and went over to him with flowers and fruit, beseeching him to come to his house with them. Guru Nanak relented, but he could not be persuaded to take up a job as his father desired, nor involve himself in the family affairs as suggested by his mother. He, however, assured his family that he would keep in touch with them, visit them occasionally and, after he had completed his mission, would come back and stay with them. His old parents were consoled and so was his dutiful spouse.

Before long, Guru Nanak left on his second mission towards the south. At Lahore, not far from Talwandi, he was visited by Duni Chand, a rich man, and his wife. Duni Chand had amassed a lot of wealth and property and lived a luxurious life. He came to Guru Nanak to pay homage to him the way the well-to-do usually propitiate both God and Mammon. As he was leaving, the Guru pulled out a needle from his pouch and gave it to Duni Chand asking him to keep it safe; he would ask for it in the next world. "But how can one carry a needle to the next world?" remarked Duni Chand. "Then what have you collected all these riches for?" asked Guru Nanak. Duni Chand and his wife heard the Guru and their eyes were opened suddenly. They went back and distributed all their wealth to the poor. They became God-fearing and, thereafter, started sharing their earnings with the needy.

Guru Nanak then visited Ajodhan (today's Pak Pattan in Pakistan), the seat of Baba Farid, the great Sufi *dervish* of the twelfth century, and met one of his successors, Shaikh Ibrahim. He had a long discourse with him. Shaikh Ibrahim recited to him the *slokas*, while Guru Nanak composed his own verses extempore to present his viewpoint. They carried on the discourse for long until Shaikh Ibrahim was fully satisfied and he said, "Guru Nanak, you have indeed found God. There is no difference between Him and you."

On his journey towards the south, Guru Nanak was accompanied by Saido and Gheho. Mardana stayed behind with his family. As he was crossing the Vindhyachal ranges, Nanak came upon a Jain temple. Its priest, called Narbhi, heard about him and came to meet him. He was aware that Guru Nanak did not believe in the exaggerated view of life in every form the way Jains do. He shot a volley of questions at the Guru: Do you eat old or new corn? Do you drink fresh or boiled water? Do you shake a tree for fruit? Who is your Guru and what power has he to save you?

Guru Nanak replied:

If the Guru is kind, devotion is perfected.
If the Guru is kind, you know no sorrow.
If the Guru is kind, pain disappears.
If the Guru is kind, you enjoy life.
If the Guru is kind, there is no fear of death.
If the Guru is kind, you remain ever happy.

If the Guru is kind, the nine treasures are obtained.
If the Guru is kind, you get to know the truth.

MAJH KI VAR (149)

The Jain priest heard this and was fully satisfied.

During his sojourn in the south, Guru Nanak went right up to Rameshwaram and Kanyakumari and across the sea to Sri Lanka. It is said that there ruled a king by the name of Shivnabh. He had heard about Guru Nanak from Mansukh, a trader from Punjab who used to visit his kingdom. Ever since the king had learnt about Guru Nanak, he longed to meet the Guru and pay him homage. Mansukh assured him that if he remembered the Guru from the core of his heart, the Guru must respond. Learning of the king's anxiety to meet his Guru, many a charlatan tried to cheat the king pretending to be Guru Nanak. He was sick of them. Then one day his courtiers told the king that Guru Nanak had indeed arrived, his prayers had been heard. But the king who had been deceived several times wouldn't believe them until he had it verified. Accordingly, he sent two most captivating dancing girls to try their charms on the visiting recluse. The moment the girls entered the premises where Guru Nanak was camping, they forgot all about their designs. They came and sat in a corner in utter devotion. The king was, in the meanwhile, waiting impatiently to know what had happened to the girls. When he learnt about their submission to the Guru, he rushed to the Guru with his courtiers and fell at his feet. Raja Shivnabh wanted

Guru Nanak to accompany him to his palace. Guru Nanak did not go. He, however, had the king put up a *dharamasala* where the devotees congregated daily, singing hymns in praise of God.

The third time Guru Nanak left home, he trekked towards the north. He was accompanied by Mardana. Guru Nanak's first halt was at Srinagar. The historical Gurudwaras at Anantnag and Mattan indicate that the Guru went even to Amarnath.

At Srinagar, Guru Nanak met a Muslim dervish known as Kamal, and a Hindu man of learning called Brahm Das. It is said that Brahm Das was very arrogant. Wherever he went, he was followed by three camels carrying the ancient works he had studied. He was fond of entering into lengthy arguments with the holy men he encountered. When he met Guru Nanak, in the first instance, he objected to his dress. Guru Nanak happened to be wearing leather shoes and a fur robe for protection against the Kashmir cold. The Guru ignored it. Brahm Das then started displaying his learning and asked Guru Nanak about the creation of the world. Guru Nanak's reply was most revealing:

For countless ages there was utter darkness;
No earth, no sky, only God's will.
No day, no night, neither the Moon nor the Sun,
He sat in trance in the void.
There was no eating, no speaking,
There was no water, no air,
No creation, no destruction,
No coming, no going,

There were no planets, no underworld,
None of the seven seas
With rivers flowing into them.
There were no planes: higher, middle or lower.
Neither hell nor heaven, nor any hour of death.
No suffering, no bliss,
No birth, no death,
No entry, no exit.
There was no Brahma, no Vishnu, no Shiva.

o o o   o o o

With His order, the world was created.
It is maintained without any support.
He created Brahma, Vishnu and Shiva.
He created also the love of Maya.
Only a few are blessed with His Word.
He watches and rules over all.
He brought about the planets, the hemisphere
   and the underworld.
And became Himself manifest.
It is the True Guru alone who imparts this
   understanding.
Says Nanak those who are truthful live in
   eternal bliss,
They are blessed with the recitation of God's Name.

MARU (1035)

Hearing this, Pandit Brahm Das was stunned. He was amazed at Guru Nanak's vision. He became Guru Nanak's disciple and decided to propagate the Word of

God. Brahm Das stayed in the valley and Kamal was advised by Guru Nanak to settle in Kurram from where he propagated the Holy Word in Kabul, Qandhar and as far as Tirah.

Leaving Srinagar, Guru Nanak penetrated the Himalayas and travelled towards Tibet. When he arrived at Lake Manasarovar, he came across a large number of *Yogis* who had escaped from oppression and chaos in the plains and had found shelter in faraway abodes in the mountains. The ascetics asked Guru Nanak about the conditions prevailing in the country. Guru Nanak chided them for running away from the hard realities of life the way they had done. He, however, told them that the times were not too happy:

> *Kaliyuga is like a dagger,*
> *Kings are butchers.*
> *Dharma has taken wings and disappeared*
> *Into the black night of falsehood;*
> *The moon of truth is nowhere to be seen.*
> *I am lost in the search,*
> *I find no way out of darkness,*
> *Afflicted with ego, I wail in sorrow,*
> *Says Nanak, how do I gain deliverance?*
>
> RAGA MAJH SLOK (145)

The ascetics, called Siddhas, entered into a long discussion with Guru Nanak. It started with prayers to the Almighty. Then followed a dialogue on how one attains union with God:

Siddhas: Can one find God by wandering in search of Him?

Nanak: Without the True Word, there is no finding Him.

Siddhas: How does one cross the ocean of the world?

Nanak: By living like a lotus or a water-bird in water. By meditating on His name and remaining free from the snare of *Maya*.

Guru Nanak recorded his discourses with various ascetics in Siddh Gosht, a long composition in the form of a dialogue in verse. It is an interesting record of the intricate metaphysical issues discussed by him. Guru Nanak has projected himself in this long composition as a seeker of God. He had three major encounters with the Siddhas: at Gorakhmata (later known as Nanakmata), at Manasarovar and at Achal Batala.

Guru Nanak's last sojourn, which he undertook after a fairly long stay at home, was towards the west. He was again accompanied by Mardana. Before he left on the journey Guru Nanak donned the blue dress of a Muslim pilgrim, took a staff in one hand and a *lota* in the other. Evidently, Guru Nanak's destination was Mecca.

On his way to Mecca, Guru Nanak had an encounter with Wali Qandhari, a dervish whose abode was on a hilltop at Hasan Abdal near Taxila, the ancient Buddhist centre.

At midday, in a wilderness, Mardana felt thirsty. Guru Nanak explained to him that there was no water in the barren rocky plateau but Mardana grew impatient. He was getting old and was like an obstinate child when he wanted something. Guru Nanak looked around and told Mardana that the nearest he could find water was on the top of the hill, the abode of the dervish Wali Qandhari.

Mardana went up the hill and asked the Muslim dervish for water. But the dervish, discovering that Mardana was a companion of Guru Nanak, refused to give him any. When Guru Nanak heard about this, he advised Mardana to go up again and make his request in all humility. "Tell him, I am the companion of Nanak, a man of God," said Guru Nanak.

But Wali Qandhari would not relent. At this, the Guru asked Mardana to go the third time and make a request for water in the name of God! Mardana scaled the hill again but was taunted by the arrogant Wali Qandhari. "He styles himself as a Guru and cannot get a drop of water for his disciple," he said.

Mardana returned, almost dead from exhaustion. Guru Nanak saw his plight and asked him to lift a slab of stone which lay a little away from them. It is said that the moment Mardana removed the slab, a spring gushed out from beneath it.

A little later when he needed water for himself, Wali Qandhari found that his well was emptying fast and that there was a stream of water flowing at the foot of the hill. Evidently, the *Yogi* had played a trick on him. In fury, Wali Qandhari rolled a boulder to crush

Guru Nanak and his companion who sat at the head of the fountain singing the praises of God. As the boulder approached Guru Nanak, he is said to have effortlessly held it back with his hand. In course of time, the place came to be known as Punja Saheb, the temple of the Holy Palm. Located in the Attock district of Pakistan, it is one of the important places of Sikh pilgrimage even today.

Arriving at Mecca, Guru Nanak felt tired. It had been a long and arduous journey to the holy city. He fell asleep and it so happened that he slept with his feet, instead of his head, towards Kaaba, the holy shrine. At midnight, a watchman on his rounds noticed this and was scandalized to find a pilgrim with his feet pointing towards the House of God. "How dare you lie with your feel pointing towards God?" he shouted. He was about to lay his corrective hands on Nanak when the Guru woke up. "Good man," he said, "I am weary after a long journey. Kindly turn my feet in the direction where God is not."

Jiwan, the watchman, was stunned. "Where God is not!" he said, his head whirling. "Where God is not!" He saw His abode in all the four directions. He had lifted Guru Nanak's feet and, rather than turning them around, lowered his head and kissed them. He washed Guru Nanak's feet with his tears. All the other pilgrims and holy men of the shrine were also moved to have Guru Nanak amidst them. They asked him many questions, "I am neither a Hindu nor a Mussalman," said Guru Nanak. "Who is superior of the two?" the pilgrims collected around him wished to know. Guru Nanak replied, "Without good deeds, neither is any good." The Guru laid stress on the love of God, humility, prayer and truthful living. He, then, recited a hymn in Persian:

I wish to make a submission, my Lord!
If you would please lend me Your ear.
You are truly a great, merciful and faultless
Sustainer.
That this world is not forever,
I am convinced.
That the messenger of death will catch hold of
me from my hair,
I am aware.
That wife, son, father and brother,
None will be able to hold my hand.
That in the end when I fall and my time to go
comes,
None would come to my rescue.
That I roam about daily given to avarice and
evil ways,
Never doing a good deed;
Such a one am I.
I am ill-omened, miserly, careless, narrow-minded
and rude.
Says Nanak, but I am Your slave,
The dust of the feet of Your minions.

TILANG (690)

The high priest of the holy shrine who, in the

meanwhile, happened to have arrived on the scene was deeply moved to hear these words.

From Mecca, Guru Nanak proceeded to Medina where he had another debate with the head priest of the shrine. What impressed people was Guru Nanak's emphasis on the unity of God and equality of man. He didn't believe in rituals. According to him only a man's good deeds and the Guru's grace earned him liberation.

At Baghdad, which he visited later, Guru Nanak made one of his most ardent devotees in a dervish who, it is said, sat for sixty long years at the foot of the slab occupied by Guru Nanak during his visit to the town.

On his way back from Mecca, Guru Nanak visited Multan. It was an important centre of Sufis in those days. As Guru Nanak was camping outside the town the dervishes in the city sent him a bowl of milk, full to the brim, indicating thereby that the place was already full of holy men. Guru Nanak put a jasmine flower in the bowl. The bowl didn't overflow; the flower floated on the milk. Guru Nanak thus spoke to the holy men of Multan in their own idiom, telling them that there was still room for a man like Nanak in their midst.

Guru Nanak then visited Saidpur (known as Eminabad in present-day Pakistan). By this time, Babar had already entered the Punjab. Guru Nanak advised his devotees in the town to leave the place and thus escape the tyranny of the marauding Mughals. Some listened to him, while others did not. As feared by Guru Nanak, Saidpur was laid waste by the invading forces soon after. Guru Nanak witnessed this heartless killing and the poet in him seems to have revolted against the divine justice. He has left some remarkable pieces of poetry describing the barbarous attack and the sufferings of the people of the Punjab:

He occupied Khurasan and subdued Hindusatan,
God don't You blame Yourself for having sent the
Mughal like a doom?
Seeing such suffering and wailing,
Didn't it hurt You Oh Lord?
You are the lone Creator of all.
If an aggressor were to kill an aggressor
I wouldn't complain.
But when a fierce lion falls on a herd of poor
cattle,
The master must take the blame.
The dogs have ruined the gem of my country,
When they die, none will ever notice them.
O God, You alone make and unmake, this is
Your greatness.
If anyone else were to style himself as great
And start doing as he pleases,
He would be like a worm feeding on a few
grains in Your eyes.
He who dies in life, he alone lives,
Says Nanak, by meditating on the Name of God.

ASA (360)

It is said that Guru Nanak, along with Mardana, was taken prisoner here. When the jailor heard him sing the divine hymn, he hastened to report the matter to the king. Babar sent for Guru Nanak to listen to his hymn. He realized that the Guru was indeed an evolved soul. He asked for his forgiveness and offered him his pouch of *bhang* by way of entertaining him as an equal, but Guru Nanak declined it, saying that he was already intoxicated with the Name of God. It was during this meeting with Babar, when Guru Nanak predicted:

> *They came in '78 and would go in '97*
> *Another hero will also rise.*

Tilang (723)

The prophecy relates to the Mughals occupying India in Samvat 1578 (a.d. 1521) and departing in Samvat 1597 (a.d. 1540). The monarch who was driven out was Humayun and the "hero" referred to is Sher Shah who had thrown him out.

Guru Nanak was now growing old. Mardana had also aged. There was still a lot to be done by way of consolidating the community. Guru Nanak's devotees all over the country and from abroad longed to visit him and sit at his feet. Accordingly, Guru Nanak decided to settle down in the Punjab. This was about a.d. 1520.

He acquired a large enough piece of land on the banks of the river Ravi. Here he set up a new township called Kartarpur — the abode of God. He gave up wearing the garb of a recluse and took to the normal dress of a Punjabi peasant. He started farming like everyone else. His wife and sons lived with him. So did Mardana and several other devotees; it was a sort of community living. Everyone was expected to work in the fields and share the harvest. There was a common kitchen. Every visitor, irrespective of caste and creed, partook of the meal offered there.

Soon after, Mardana's end came. Guru Nanak advised Mardana's son Shahzada not to wail and lament the loss of his father because he had returned to his heavenly home; there is no mourning for the blessed souls. After his father died, Shahzada joined Guru Nanak as his *rabab* player.

One day, Guru Nanak was working in the fields when he saw a horse-rider heading towards him. "I am Lehna," said the stranger, leaving his horse at a respectable distance and approaching the Guru in all humility. Guru Nanak looked at his face and observed, "So you have arrived, Lehna the creditor, I have been waiting for you all these days. I must pay off your debt." ("Lehna" in Punjabi means debt or creditor.)

Lehna didn't understand what was said but he was charmed by Guru Nanak's person. He had heard a great deal about him from one of Guru Nanak's devotees, Bhai Jodha, who lived in Khadur, the village to which Lehna belonged.

Lehna was the son of a well-to-do businessman who was a great devotee of Durga. He went to the shrine of the goddess in Kangra, every year. The more he heard about Guru Nanak and his *bani* (utterances) from Bhai Jodha, the more he longed to meet him. At last he could restrain himself no longer and, leading a party of pilgrims to the Kangra shrine of the deity, he left them midway and came to Kartarpur. Once he had met Guru

Nanak there was no looking back. He served the master day and night. Before long he became the most trusted disciple of the Guru. Lehna's devotion to Guru Nanak was absolute. He served him as none else did, not even his two sons.

It is said that once Guru Nanak, accompanied by Lehna and his two sons, came across something covered with a sheet of cloth that looked like a corpse. "Who would eat it?" asked Guru Nanak unexpectedly. His sons were astonished to hear these words. They thought something had gone wrong with their father. "Master, if it pleases you, I'll do it," said Lehna and moving ahead removed the cover to find that it was a tray of sacred food. Lehna offered it first to Guru Nanak and his sons and then partook of the leftovers himself. Guru Nanak was most touched to see this. He said:

> Lehna, you were blessed with the sacred food because you could share it with others. If the people use the wealth bestowed on them by God for themselves alone or for treasuring it, it is like a corpse. But if they decide to share it with others, it becomes sacred food. You have known the secret. You are my image.

Then, Guru Nanak blessed Lehna with his *ang* (hand) and gave him a new name – Angad. Angad was a changed man. He became a part of Guru Nanak's body and soul, as it were.

A few days later Pir Bahauddin, a high priest from Multan, visited Guru Nanak. He said, "My end is near,

I have come to seek your blessings so that my journey to the next world is smooth." Hearing this Guru Nanak observed that he, too, would soon follow him.

Soon after Guru Nanak held a special meeting for which devotees gathered from far and near. Amidst the chanting of hymns, Nanak invited Angad formally to occupy the seat of the Guru. Thus, ordaining Angad as his successor, he retired. While everyone present hailed the new Guru, members of Guru Nanak's family were not happy over the decision. They felt that the sons had been deprived of their right to succession. According to Guru Nanak, hereditary privilege was not what made a Guru; the one who deserved it most was chosen.

One day Guru Nanak was found reciting:

> *The auspicious hour has arrived,*
> *Come and pour the ceremonial oil.*
> *Bless me, O friends, so that I meet my Master,*
> *Every home gets such tidings; these calls are*
> *received daily.*
> *Says Nanak, the caller must be remembered,*
> *The auspicious hour has arrived.*

SOHILA (12)

Guru Nanak said his prayers after his bath and lay down, covering himself with a sheet of cloth. The light that showed the path to millions then merged into the eternal light. It was a day like any other day; having completed his mission, Guru Nanak passed away quietly.

It is said his Muslim devotees built a mausoleum in his memory and his Hindu disciples a *samadhi* on the banks of the river Ravi. Soon both were washed away by the changing course of the river, leaving behind the fragrant memory dear to both Hindus and Muslims. The people of the Punjab remembered him as:

> Baba Nanak, the great man of God!
> The Guru of the Hindus and the *Pir* of the Mussalmans.

He is remembered as such even today by Hindus and Muslims alike.

While there is no definitive biography of Guru Nanak, there have been a number of attempts at writing the story of his life by his devotees soon after his passing away. Historians might reject a great deal of these writings as sheer adulation, born of excessive devotion, but these accounts do provide the essential landmarks and help us structure a fairly reliable picture of the Guru's life and times.

Unlike Mahavira and Buddha, Guru Nanak has left behind a vast treasure of his utterances in verse (*Gurubani*), carefully compiled in the *Guru Granth Sahib*. It is not difficult to imagine what sort of a soul the author of these writings was. Not only this, the poetical work bequeathed to us by Guru Nanak inevitably contains copious references to his times, to the places he visited, the people he met and the discourses he delivered.

In his book, *A Life-sketch of Guru Nanak*, Dr. Hari Ram Gupta says:

At the time of Guru Nanak's advent, both the prevailing religions _ Hinduism and Islam _ had become corrupt and degraded. They had lost their pristine purity and glory. The Vedas were unintelligible to the people and had been replaced by Tantric literature . . . caste had grown rigid and had split into numerous sub-castes . . . Similar was the state of affairs in Islam . . . Political conditions were much worse . . .

Men of vision were worried about the prevailing state of affairs. They attacked the rot that had set in in their society from various angles. The Bhakti movement, the Sufi cult and the Sant tradition attempted a synthesis of the Hindu and the Muslim ways of life and all the three had dedicated men from among Hindus and Muslims to give them direction. Rather than concern themselves with the political and economic issues, these sects devoted their attention to social problems, trying their best to restore man's faith in God. They believed that once man turned his face towards God, the other maladies society suffered from would be easy to cure.

By and large, Guru Nanak can be said to have belonged to the Bhakti movement. Bhakti means loving devotion. In the case of Guru Nanak, this devotion was towards God, the Supreme Being. Its expression is strictly through meditation and through living a truthful life in the image of God.

The Bhakti movement in Northern India was a revolt against the ritualism, casteism and formalism of the

Brahmans among the Hindus, and the *Mullas* and *Qazis* among the Muslims. It had its roots in the cult of Vaishnava bhakti which came from the south, the ancient tradition of Tantric yoga as practised by the Nath sect of yogis and the Sufi orders of Islam. It rejected all exterior forms of worship, ceremonies, pilgrimages and ritual bathing. No importance was attached to celibacy or asceticism. Guru Nanak himself married and had two sons. Towards the close of his life, he came to settle down at Kartarpur, where he tended his crops and ran a community kitchen which was shared by high and low, rich and poor.

Faith was the pre-requisite for the Bhakti movement; without faith there could be no love. The devotee does not question the will of God; he carries out His dictates. He does not feel elated in comfort nor depressed in trouble. The ways of God are inscrutable.

> *The Guru's Word in the heart is the earring of*
> *the yogi*
> *And humility the garb of the recluse*
> *Acceptance of His will is eternal bliss.*

A<small>SA</small>

Devotion also entails complete surrender to God, an unconditional submission. The devotee is like a bride who must surrender herself completely to her lord to enjoy the bliss of married life. God is the bridegroom and the whole world is a bride.

> *Go and ask the bride, how she won her*
> *lord's heart.*

Do as he desires and shed all conceit.
He who bestowes the bliss of loving devotion
Alone should be adored.
Carry out his commands,
Surrender to him body and soul
Says the bride, this is how you win your lord.

TILANG (722)

Love of God is not possible without the fear of
God. One fears most whom one loves best. The *bhakta*
recognizes the immensity of the authority of God
absolutely. The entire world created by God lives in His
fear.

In fear the winds ever blow,
In fear millions of rivers flow,
In fear the fire does its job,
In fear the earth is heavy under its weight,
In fear the moon moves on its head,
Even the God of Death lives in fear.

ASA (469)

Real devotion is God's love. It can be of two types:
outward (*laukik*) and inward (*anuraga*). Guru Nanak
rejected outward devotion. He laid stress on inward
devotion or pure love. He did not believe in dancing
and jumping or the other antics of the yogis and the
Sufis of his time.

The devotees play on the accompaniments
and the gurus dance,

They move their feet
and shake their heads.
The dust rises and settles on their hair,
people see it and laugh.
They do this only to earn their livelihood.

ASA (465)

The Bhakta sings God's praises day and night. By singing His praises, he can hope to be like Him. By singing His praises, one can hope to find favour in the Lord's court.

There is no end to God's praises;
Of those who praise Him there is no end.

JAPUJI

There are nine forms of Bhakti accepted in the spiritual order. These are: 1. Listening (*shrawan*), 2. music (*kirtan*), 3. remembrance (*simuran*), 4. following in the footsteps of the master (*padsevan*), 5. service (*archan*), 6. singing praises (*vandana*), 7. obedience (*dasbhav*), 8. friendship (*mitrata*) and 9. self-surrender (*atma nivedan*). Guru Nanak subscribed to all these but the best form of Bhakti according to him is *prema Bhakti*, loving devotion to God.

According to Guru Nanak, the love of God follows the love of man. Only they can love God who love their fellowmen. At times it is through the love of man that one finds the love of God.

Guru Nanak broke the barriers of caste. In his eyes, there was no higher or lower caste. He rejected the privileges acquired by birth. He fraternized with the poor and the down-trodden, the peasant and the worker. The whole world was one family for him. He respected other religions. He spoke many languages. He dressed like a Turk or Pathan while visiting their respective countries. In his own country, he clad himself like an *Udasi*, in the saffron robes of a *yogi*, the ordinary dress of a Punjabi Khatri or the garb of a Sufi mystic, as it pleased him.

Guru Nanak never made promises of paradise and heavenly luxuries as a reward for ritualistic practices. He did not offer future bliss as a bait for religious living – no houries, no rivulets of honey, no springs of milk. He assured people peace and harmony in this world in return for a truthful life and ethically correct social behaviour.

Except, of course, in the places of pilgrimages which he visited as a seeker of truth, Guru Nanak never cared to stay in temples, mosques or other shrines while visiting a town; he did not prefer conventional places of worship for preaching his message. The blue dome of the sky was his cover and he talked about his new way of life in the open. His meetings were open to anyone who cared to attend. If he had to choose he would stay with people like Sajjan, the cheat, who needed him – to show them light, and put them on the path of righteousness.

Guru Nanak combined in himself a recluse, an ascetic and a family man who married and had children.

He was the fond brother of a doting sister. He was a dutiful husband and a loving father. And yet, he was unduly attached to none. For years, he would go out towards the east, west, north and south, but every time he would come back to his home. He promised his sister Nanaki that he would come to her whenever she remembered him. It is said that once when the sister in Nanaki got the better of her and she wished in her heart of hearts to have a glimpse of her brother, Guru Nanak did, to her great joy, keep his promise. He also ensured that his wife was suitably provided for and his sons were brought up properly. His parents took a little longer to appreciate the unconventional ways of their only son.

During the last twenty years of his life, Guru Nanak made an experiment that was unique for his times. He had one of his well-to-do devotees part with a large enough piece of land and had a new town built thereon. It was called Kartarpur, the abode of the Creator. It was the first ever experiment in community living in our part of the world. The land was common, the farming was common, and there was a common kitchen; Guru Nanak insisted on the common kitchen, so that the curse of the caste system could be removed from his society. The Hindus of the day were obsessed with the caste system which had acquired rigidity over the ages. The Muslims had also contracted it, to some extent, from the Hindus. Nobody could see him unless he had eaten in the common kitchen. It is said that Guru Nanak also farmed along with others in the fields. He attached great importance to manual labour. Before long,

Kartarpur became a flourishing town with lush, green fields, laden with rich crops. Guru Nanak's devotees came from far and near to pay homage to the Master at Kartarpur where Guru Nanak lived with his wife and the two sons.

When the time came for Guru Nanak to nominate a successor, he felt that neither of his sons had come up to his expectations. Here was the greatest test of his life. His sons had aspired to become the Guru. One of them had never married and lived the life of an ascetic. Guru Nanak did not approve it. He attached greater importance to normal family life. He, therefore, ordained one of his followers who had come to stay with him as the next Guru. This peeved his two sons, one of whom started his own sect. But the stewardship of the Sikhs remained with Guru Angad, who became the second Sikh Guru.

Guru Nanak's three important precepts were: There is no Hindu or Mussalman: one must work and share one's earnings; and an active life is superior to a life of sheer contemplation.

It is no wonder that his followers weathered many storms and have continued to remain in the forefront of progressive forces. They are a hard-working people, devoted and self-sacrificing.

Guru Nanak's hymns remain a perennial source of inspiration for them.

Proud to be a Poet

Guru Nanak, as mentioned earlier, was proud to be a poet. More than once he called himself "Nanak the poet". Almost all his compositions have his name figuring in the last couplet according to the poetic tradition of his time. And what a fine poet he was! The like of him in Punjabi is yet to be born. His writing remains unsurpassed. He has 958 compositions to his credit. They contain also the longer works like the *Japuji, Barah Mah* and *Siddh Gosht.* These are not only exquisite poetry; almost all of them can be sung to music. The poet Guru Nanak did not only respect the traditional forms, he was the most modern and remains so even among the modernists of today. His verse conforms to conversational rhythms and varies its pace according to the mood of the text.

During Guru Nanak's times the means of communication were forbidding and messages were carried by word of mouth from town to town and from village to village. Guru Nanak undertook long journeys during which his companion Mardana played on the *rabab.* Guru Nanak poured out inspired words in some of his finest poetry. With illiteracy rampant around him, it was on purpose that Guru Nanak chose this medium to propagate his message. He also endeavoured to set up cells called *manjis* where those who subscribed to his way of life assembled for meditation and recitation of hymns. In due course, there was a network of these cells throughout India, and beyond its borders in Sri Lanka, across the Himalayas and in West Asia.

The poets of the Bhakti movement had rejected Sanskrit as well as Persian, the languages of the elite, and chose to communicate in the language of the people to whom they belonged. Namdev, Ravidas, Kabir, some of the predecessors of Guru Nanak, belonged to the so-called lower classes of their society — Namdev was a washerman, Ravidas was a cobbler and Kabir was a weaver. Guru Nanak himself was not a Brahmin, but a Khatri (Kshatriya).

The protagonists of the Bhakti movement not only evolved a link language called Sadhukari, spoken and popularized by the saint-poets in Northern India, but also adopted the poetic forms which were popular with the common people. Their metres and measures followed the folk songs and folk ballads that the common people were familiar with. They drew their similes from the everyday life of the common man. They employed familiar symbols though with a freshness of their own.

Almost all the poetry that Guru Nanak wrote can be sung to music. The text conforms to specific ragas prevalent in the classical Hindustani music of the day. Where Guru Nanak followed the better-known musical forms of folk ballads, he made it a point to mention the fact at the beginning of the composition; that it was designed to be sung in such and such tune in the style of such and such ballad. For instance, in the opening of *Asa di Var*, a longish work sung by the Sikh community every morning as a divine service, it is stated:

"The *Var* with slokas is written by the first Guru (Nanak) and should be sung to the tune of *Tunda Asraja.*"

Guru Nanak's Masterpiece

Amongst Guru Nanak's longer works, *Japuji* is the best

known. It is one of the finest compositions in our literature. Had Guru Nanak not been the evolved soul that he was, he would still have ranked amongst the greatest souls of the world on account of his authorship of this work alone.

According to Mehrban, one of his three early biographers, the *Japuji* was composed after Guru Nanak's communion with God when he disappeared in Bain at Sultanpur. This appears at best to be a conjecture, as most of Mehrban's account of Guru Nanak's life evidently is. Mehrban made an attempt to reconstruct the story of Guru Nanak's life, based upon his *bani*. He naturally gave the *Japuji* the premier place, supposedly uttered in God's own presence, during Guru Nanak's first mystic experience. According to another source, a manuscript in the Punjab University library at Lahore, believed to have been written in mid-seventeenth century, the *Japuji* was composed at Kartarpur after Lehna had joined Guru Nanak. While there is little evidence of the period of its composition, considering the maturity and sweep of thought and the consummate skill with which it is constructed, the *Japuji* appears to have been written during the latter part of Guru Nanak's life, most probably after he had settled down at Kartarpur.

While Guru Nanak conformed to the traditional pattern, with an invocation to God in the beginning and a summing-up in the form of an epilogue at the end, there is evidence of a great deal of ingenuity and poetic skill in the body of the composition. The poet Guru Nanak never cared for rigidity of poetic forms. Like the modern poets, he varied his metres and rhymes according to the flow of his thought and the content of his message.

In the invocation, he describes God in vivid terms but with utmost economy of words. A clever craftsman, Guru Nanak employs negative images also to make his picture precise and clear. He affirms the unity of God most emphatically:

> *There is but one God*
> *Truth is His name*
> *He is the Master-Creator.*
> *He is unafraid.*
> *He disdains none.*
> *He is the Image-Eternal.*
> *He is beyond incarnation.*
> *He is self-existent.*
> *He is realised through the grace of the True Guru.*
>
> JAPUJI (1)

God cannot be known by just thinking about Him. He cannot be known by solemn silence, nor deep meditation. Fasting has its virtues, but the thirst for truth cannot be quenched by it. God can't be reached by any other way: It is only the righteous path that leads man to God.

The aforesaid is how the Japuji opens after the formal invocation. The rest of the poem is an answer to the following question posed by the poet in the first hymn:

> *How then shall the truth be known?*
> *How is the veil of false illusion torn?*

Guru Nanak goes on to provide the answer. Despite the limitations of poetry, the dissertation is highly lucid and cogent.

There are thirty-eight hymns in the *Japuji*, exclusive of the invocation and the concluding *sloka*.

The first seven hymns suggest that in order to narrow down the gap between God and man, created by *Maya*, one must submit to the will of God. And, having fashioned the way of life as ordained by Him, one should sing His praises. One becomes like him whom one emulates. Guru Nanak repeatedly reminds us that without the grace of God, we cannot accept His will or even sing His praises. By His grace alone are some saved and some others are doomed to die without it. Actions determine how we are born but it is His grace which secures our salvation.

The next four hymns (8-11) are devoted to the virtues of listening to the Word of God. By listening to the Word, man becomes wise, saintly, courageous and contented. By listening to the Word, man conquers the fear of death, and his sins and sorrows disappear. By listening to the Word, man learns the truth, his mind is led to meditation and there is no need to go on pilgrimages.

Another set of four hymns (12-15) dwells on those who, having listened to His Word, believe in God. Guru Nanak says that the bliss of the believer is indescribable. The believer gains the knowledge of all the spheres. He understands the ways of God, attains salvation and saves his kith and kin.

In the following four hymns (16-19), Guru Nanak says that believers become leaders of men and are honoured in the eyes of God. But it is difficult to follow the mysteries of the Divine; the more one goes into them, the deeper they tend to become. There are countless men who pray and adore God, and those who worship Him and undergo penance. Similarly, there are countless fools and thieves and frauds. Man has no power to give praise to God. It is His wish that prevails.

Some of the more important observations in the next eight hymns (20-27) are:

> As soiled garments are washed with soap, the soul dirtied with sin is cleansed with prayer.
> It is our actions and not words that make us sinners or saints.
> Pilgrimage, austerity, compassion and generosity are like mustard seeds compared with the virtues of one who listens to, believes in and cherishes the Word of God.
> Nobody knows when the world was created; the Pandit, the *Qazi*, or the Yogi too does not; only He who made it can tell.
> God alone can measure His greatness; he who would know His height must be as tall as He.
> He is the king of kings who is granted grace and the power to praise.
> It is difficult to say how priceless God is, those who know Him are mute with adoration.

The next four hymns (28-31) are a salutation to the Primal and Pure Entity, who has no beginning and no end. He has a unique form which endures forever.

The following three hymns (32-34) maintain that it is the grace of God that is all important. God has the pride of power, He is true and He dispenses truth.

The last four hymns (35-38) describe the various stages before man achieves union with God. The first is the realm of just and truthful living and correct behaviour. Then man attains the realm of knowledge, where reason is supreme. In the realm of grace that follows, nothing but His blessings avail. The highest is the realm of God, the truth which is gained only by His grace and blessings.

The summing-up asserts that not only do the toils of those who worship God end, but they also set others free:

> *Air is the Guru, water the father*
> *And earth is the mother-superior.*
> *Day and night are the nursemaids*
> *With whom the whole world plays.*
> *Dharamraj sitting in the Lord's Court*
> *Watches our good and bad deeds.*
> *Depending upon our actions*
> *We get close to or move away from God.*
> *Those who remember Him*
> *Their labours bear fruit.*
> *Says Nanak, they've bright faces,*
> *They ferry others along with them.*

JAPUJI (8)

The composition is most appropriately titled *Japuji* since it emphasises the repetition of the name of God. His adoration is the only remedy to bridge the gap between man and the Divine force created by falsehood. The prayer endears one to God. His love earns one bliss, which is the supreme fulfilment.

Ernst Trumpp, an Indologist commissioned to translate the Holy Granth, gave up the task midway complaining that there was far too much repetition in the scriptural text. There is much truth in this. However, when the theme remains the same — concern for the Divine — and there is a plurality of pens handling it, repetition can seldom be obviated. The reader of Guru Nanak may also find repetition in his hymns. While reasserting the eternal truths, the inevitability of it becomes a stern reality. But the poet Guru Nanak rescues it splendidly with his varied imagery, sensitivity of expression and ambience in which the utterances occur.

Guru Nanak's approach to life is invariably affirmative. He is supremely alert to the vital importance of existence. He tries consistently to find his real self with its multiplicity intact. An extraordinarily complex poet who writes simply, he skilfully holds together strains of intricate and elusive thought. Every word that he uttered evinced his awareness of the mission which, it seems, he received from the Divine Entity with his genius. Considering the vision and sweep of his hymns, it is no wonder that Guru Nanak was hailed as a Prophet by Sikhs and non-Sikhs alike.

Japuji

(The Sikh Morning Prayer)

There is but one God.
Truth is His name.
He is the Master-Creator.
He is unafraid.
He disdains none.
He is the Image-Eternal.
He is beyond incarnation.
He is self-existent.
He is realised through the grace of the True
    Guru.

Japu

He was here in the beginning,
And before the beginning.
He is here today,
He will be here hereafter.

If you were to meditate on Him,

You may not succeed
Even if you tried a hundred thousand times.
If you tried to take to silence,
You may not succeed
Even if you meditated on Him ever and ever.
A hungry man's hunger remains unquenched
Even if he were to amass the entire
world's wealth.
You may try a million means
Not one will succeed.
Then how can one be truthful?
How can one tear down the wall of falsehood?
Do as He bids you to do,
This is what Nanak has to state. (1)

In His pleasure are formed the figures.
Nobody knows what pleases Him.
If He pleases, He infuses life in them.
If He pleases, He bestows honour upon them.
The high and the low are created at His
pleasure.
At His pleasure one suffers weal or woe.
Some are pardoned at His pleasure
Others, under His orders, run the course of
transmigration.
Everyone is subject to His command.
Those who abide by His bidding
They Suffer not from self-conceit, says Nanak. (2)

Those who are mighty
Sing of His might.

Those who are blessed with them
Sing of His bounties.
Some sing of His virtues,
His greatness and His charming ways.
They sing of His learning
Who are erudite.
Some remember Him as Creator
And also as One who torches the body to ashes.
Some adore Him as He who takes life away
And then restores it if it pleases Him so.
Some find Him seemingly far far away,
Some find Him face-to-face for ever.
There is no end to them
Who sing His tales.
They have narrated millions and millions of them.
The Lord continues to bestow favours,
The recipients get weary.
For ages and ages
The partakers have partaken of His provisions.
Through His command, He puts them on the
*   right path.*
Says Nanak, the Lord beyond care beholds
And feels pleased. (3)

He is the True Lord,
Truth is His name.
His language, limitless love.
They ask and implore,
The Giver ever gives.
What do I offer to behold His court?
What prayer do I make

That He takes kindly to me?
In the ambrosial hours of the morning
Remember and revere Him.
You are born as per your karma.
His grace alone gives you salvation.
Says Nanak, this is the way to know Him,
The Truthful pervades everywhere. (4)

He can neither be created
Nor can He be established.
The Immaculate Lord is evolved from Himself.
Those who serve Him are glorified.
Says Nanak, we must sing His praises,
The One who is the vast treasure-house of
      virtues.
We should sing and listen to His praises,
And adore Him in the heart.
Thus would we be relieved of pain
And carry pleasure home.
The Guru-conscious lives with the Divine Word.
The Guru-conscious is master of the Vedas.
The Guru-conscious remains merged in the Lord.
The Guru is Shiva, the Guru is Vishnu,
The Guru is Brahma, the Guru is Parvati.
Even if I know, I dare not talk about Him.
He cannot be contained in words.
The Guru has revealed the secret to me;
He is the Provider of all living beings.
May I never forget Him! (5)

If it pleases Him,
I bathe at the places of pilgrimage.
If it pleases Him not,
It's no use taking holy dips.
He has created all the world, I behold
But without Karma nothing can be had.
There are gems, jewels and rubies in one's lot,
Only if one heeds the Guru's Word.
The Guru has revealed to me the secret:
All the human beings have only one Provider.
May I never forget Him! (6)

Even if you are as old as four ages,
Or ten times older than that.
Even if you are known in the nine continents,
And everyone follows you around.
Even if you've earned a good name
And the world sings your praises.
If He doesn't take notice of you,
Nobody will give you any quarter.
He provides the minutest worm,
Even the sinners attribute their sins to Him.
Says Nanak, He bestows merits on them who
*   have none;*
The meritorious, of course, owe their merits to
*   Him.*
I can think of none who can do Him good. (7)

Hearkening to His name
Makes one a siddha, pir or super yogi.
Hearkening to His name

Enlightens one about the earth, its support and
    the sky.
Hearkening to His Name
Enlightens one about continents, the upper and
    the lower Worlds.
Hearkening to His Name
Death dare not essay one.
Says Nanak, the devotees are ever in bliss.
Hearkening to His Name
Relieves one of suffering and sin. (8)

Hearkening to His Name
One becomes Shiva, Brahma and Indra.
Hearkening to His Name
Even slanderers start praising.
Hearkening to His Name
Reveals secrets Divine and those of the body.
Hearkening to His Name is hearing
The Shastras, the Smritis and the Vedas.
Says Nanak, devotees are ever in bliss.
Hearkening to His Name
Relieves one of suffering and sin. (9)

Hearkening to His Name
Makes one truthful, contented and enlightened.
Hearkening to His Name
Is like bathing at the sixty-eight places of
    pilgrimage.
Hearkening to His Name
Is reading and gaining glory.
Hearkening to His Name

Is composing one's mind and meditating on Him.
Says Nanak, the devotees are ever in bliss.
Hearkening to His Name
Relieves from suffering and sin. (10)

Hearkening to His Name
One dives deep into the ocean of virtue.
Hearkening to His Name
Makes one a sheikh, pir *or* sultan.
Hearkening to His Name
The blind find the path.
Hearkening to His Name
The Limitless comes within one's reach.
Says Nanak, devotees are ever in bliss.
Hearkening to His Name
Relieves one of suffering and sin. (11)

He who follows Him,
The Lord is beyond even his conjecture.
He who tries it
Has to regret it.
The paper and pen can scribe it not.
They sit and ponder over it.
Such is the Name of my untainted Lord,
He who accepts Him alone understands Him. (12)

He who follows Him
Is awakened and becomes knowledgeable.
He who follows Him
Has awareness of all the spheres.
He who follows Him,

Never comes to grief.
He who follows Him,
Is free from the fear of death.
Such is the Name of my Immaculate Lord,
He who accepts Him alone understands Him. (13)

He who follows Him
Doesn't ever lose his way.
He who follows Him
Is held everywhere in esteem.
He who follows Him,
Treads the path unafraid.
He who follows Him
Is wedded to Dharma.
Such is the Name of my Immaculate Lord,
He who accepts Him alone understands Him. (14)

He who follows Him
Gets to the gate of salvation.
He who follows Him
Is saved along with his kin.
He who follows Him
Cruises also the devotees of the Guru.
He who follows Him
Doesn't have to beg of others.
Such is the Name of my Immaculate Lord,
He who accepts Him alone understands
   Him. (15)

The elect are acceptable.
The elect are supreme.

The elect are honoured in the Court of the Lord.
The elect are the glory of the King's portals.
The elect look upon the Guru alone.
If one were to sit and ponder over it,
The Creator's favours are too many to count:
Son of Compassion, Dharma *is the* Dhaval*
Who is installed with the skill of Patience.
He who understands the extent of the load on
    the shoulders of the Dhaval *is truly learned.*
The earth is spread far and farther away;
What must it need to support its load!
God's ever felicitous pen records
Names and species of all His flock.
Few can maintain this account.
If one were to keep a count of the numbers,
One will have to write for ever.
Who can figure
Your might and charm
And Your favours?
With one word You created the Universe,
And millions of rivers began to flow.
No one can imagine Your greatness, Lord!
I am sacrifice unto You not once.
Whatever pleases You is the right pursuit.
You are the Eternal, Formless One. (16)

Countless are those who meditate on You.
Countless are those who adore You.
Countless are those who worship You.

---

* The mythical bull

Countless are those who practise penance.
Countless are scriptures, oral and written.
Countless are yogis, weary at heart.
Countless are bhaktas who reflect on Your
virtues.
Countless are the truthful and countless are the
charitable.
Countless are the heroes who can bear the blows
of steel.
Countless remain silent to contemplate on You.
No one can ever estimate Your greatness,
I am sacrifice unto You not once.
Whatever pleases You is the right pursuit.
You are the Eternal, Formless One. (17)

Countless are fools, utterly blind.
Countless are thieves, defrauding others.
Countless live by the strength of their muscle.
Countless are cut-throats, countless are killers.
Countless are sinners given to evil.
Countless are liars who lean on falsehood.
Countless are aliens used to the food forbidden.
Countless are slanderers loaded with sin.
Nanak, the humble has reflected and observed:
I am sacrifice unto You not once,
Whatever pleases You is the right pursuit,
You are the Eternal, Formless one. (18)

Countless are Your Names and countless abodes.
Unfathomable realms, out of reach.
Counting the Countless is an impossible task.

It is with the Word that You are remembered.
It is with the Word that You are adored.
It is with the Word that one sings Your songs.
It is the Word that enables one to read and
 write.
It is the Word that determines one's destiny.
And He who writes figures nowhere.
Whatever You order the mortal must accept.
You are known as great, as great You are.
There is hardly a place without Your Name.
What power have I to ponder over You?
I am sacrifice unto You not once.
Whatever pleases You is the right pursuit.
You are the Eternal, Formless One. (19)

If hands, feet and the body are soiled,
The dirt can be washed with water.
If clothes are dirtied with waste matter,
They can be cleaned by applying soap.
If the mind is made filthy with sin,
It can be tidied with the dye of His Name.
Mere words don't make the virtuous or the vicious.
It is deeds that you carry with you.
You must reap what you have sown,
Nanak comes and goes as per His command. (20)

Visits to temples, ascetic practices, compassion
 and charity
Gain you but a sesame seed of credit.
It is hearkening to His Name, accepting and
 adoring Him

That obtains emancipation by bathing in the
*   shrine of the soul.*
All virtues are Yours O Lord!
I have none;
Without good deeds one cannot even meditate.
Everything pleasing reflects You
As the varied scriptures.
Truth and beauty keep the mind excited ever.
What was the hour, what the moment, what the
*   lunar day and what the weekday,*
What was the season and what the month
When the world was created?
Pandits know not the hour
If it is stated at all in the Puranas.
Nor do the qazis if it is written in the Qur'an.
The yogis, too, are not aware of the lunar or
*   weekday*
Nor about the season or month.
It is the Creator who has created the world,
He alone knows about it.
How do I say, how adore, how describe and
*   how realise?*
Says Nanak, everyone tries to say something,
Each one appears wiser than the other.
God is great, His Name is great,
Whatever happens is ordained by Him.
Says Nanak, if we were to pretend a claim on
*   gnosis,*
We would not be happy hereafter. (21)

There are nether worlds beneath the nether
    world,
And millions of skies above the sky.
That they are weary of the search
The Vedas say with one voice.
The Islamic scriptures claim
That there are eighteen thousand worlds.
But the fact remains that God is one.
Had there been a record,
One would write about it.
They who tried to find it out, died in the search.
He whom Nanak calls Great
Alone knows all about Himself. (22)

Admirers eulogise Him.
Yet they know Him not a bit.
The way the rivers and streams
Know not the ocean in which they merge.
The ocean, the sovereign, the mountain with its
    precious treasure
Are like worms
For the one who forgets not his Name. (23)

There is no end to the Lord's praises.
There is no end to those who sing them.
There is no end to the workers.
There is no end to the givers.
There is no end to His beholders.
There is no end to His hearers.
No one knows my Lord's mind.
No one knows the limits of His creation.

There is no end to the boundaries of the limit.
To know the limit many bewail.
No one knows where the limits end;
This limit no one knows.
The more one talks about Him,
The greater He appears.
The Master is great, His seat is high;
Higher and higher still is His status.
One has to be as great to realise His greatness;
How great He is,
He alone knows.
Says Nanak, His grace and one's Karma help
*   obtain*
His bounty. (24)

Your bounties are too many,
They are beyond my count;
You are a great Giver
Without a shade of malice.
Many ask for unsurpassed valour,
There is no end to those who ponder over you,
There are many who die in idle pursuits,
There are those who receive gifts and
*   acknowledge not,*
There are ever so many fools who keep on
*   eating and wasting,*
There are those who suffer distress and privation
*   and remain afflicted,*
This, too, is Your munificence, my Lord!
Emancipation is Your privilege to grant,
None else dare assume it.

If anyone else dare try and intervene,
He should know the disgrace in store for him.
He knows Himself and Himself He gives.
Even then not many accept the fact
He on whom He bestows His praise,
Says Nanak, he is the king of kings. (25)

Priceless are Your virtues and priceless
    Your conduct.
Priceless are Your clients and priceless the
    wares.
Priceless are those who make purchases.
Priceless is Your devotion and priceless getting
    absorbed in it.
Priceless is Your dharma and priceless the
        court where it is administered.
Priceless are measures and priceless the weights.
Priceless the benevolence and priceless
        your decisions.
You are beyond any price; above evaluation.
Those who tried to find; they merged in You.
They recognise You who study the Vedas and the
    Puranas.
Scholars recognise You as do the learned
    speakers.
You are recognised by Brahma and Indra as
    well.
The milkmaids recognise You and also their god
    Krishna.
Shiva recognises You and also the siddhas.

*And all the Buddhas created by You
    recognise You.*
*The demi-gods recognise you as those who serve
    in silence do.*
There are far too many who recognise You.
There are those who do so and depart.
If You were to create as many more
*They would even then not be able to describe
    fully Your virtues.*
You become great, as great You would like to be.
Says Nanak, the True Lord alone knows about it.
If someone were to boast about it,
*He would be deemed the most foolish among
    fools.* (26)

What is the gate like,
What is the house like,
Where You dwell and watch over us?
Where countless instruments are played,
Where numerous singers sing.
There is no end of musical measures
Presented by fairy-like faces.
The air, the water, the fire sing Your praises,
Dharamraja adores You waiting at Your gate,
His scribes sing Your praises,
And those who keep just records.
Ishwar, Brahma and Devi sing Your praises,
Those whom You have honoured.
Indra sings Your praises adorning his throne
*Along with other gods gathered at Your
    threshold.*

Ascetics sing Your praises sitting in meditation,
And the sages in their contemplation.
They sing Your praises
Who are continent, truthful and contented.
And the mighty heroes.
Sing the pandits and the learned yogis
Who have read the Vedas for ages.
Your praises are sung by the charming beauties
Who beguile heaven, the nether world and the
    world in between.
All the gems of men created by You
Sing Your praises at the sixty-eight places of
    pilgrimage.
Your praises are sung by warriors and the great
    heroes
Together with all those born from the four
    sources of creation.
The entire world, the planets and the solar
    system
Created and maintained by You
Sing Your praises.
They sing Your praises whom You love.
As those who are Your disciples and devoted to
    You.
And several others sing Your praises
Whom I cannot recall,
They are beyond Nanak's reckoning.
He is the eternal True Lord,
His name is Truth.
He is there,
He will be there.

He doesn't go, nor will He ever go,
He who has conceived this world,
He who has created several species of various
  kinds.
Great as He is
He looks after His creation.
He does what He pleases,
No one may order Him about.
He is the king, the King of kings.
Says Nanak, He does what He desires. (27)

Let contentment be the earrings, modesty your
  beggar's pouch
And meditation your ashes.
Let the fear of death be your head-dress,
Your transparency that of a virgin,
And the faith in God your staff.
Let your sect be the brotherhood of man
And the conquest of the self your conquest of
  the world.
I salute the one who is
Primal, Pure, Without Beginning and Indestructible,
Remaining in the same form from age to age. (28)

Let Knowledge Divine be your food,
  compassion your steward
And the celestial melody ring in your mind.
He alone is the Master who reigns supreme,
Riches and miracles have no attraction for Him.
Union and separation are both His gifts;
One gets what is in one's destiny.

I salute the One who is:
Primal, Pure, Without Beginning and
    Indestructible,
Remaining in the same form from age to age. (29)

There is but one Mother with a plan of propagation.
She has appointed three agents.
One* creates, the other** sustains
And the third⁺ is there to kill.
He runs the show as He pleases,
Everything happens as He commands.
He beholds everyone while the latter can't see Him.
It is a great mystery!
I salute the One who is
Primal, Pure, Without Beginning and Indestructible,
Remaining in the same form from age to age. (30)

God's seat and His provision stores are to be
    found all over.
Whatever you see was created at one stroke.
Having created, the Creator watches His creation.
Says Nanak, whatever the True Lord does is
    truthful.
I salute the One who is
Primal, Pure, Without Beginning and Indestructible,
Remaining in the same form from age to age. (31)

---

*   Brahma
**   Vishnu
+   Shiva

From one tongue, let there be a hundred
    thousand tongues
And then twenty times more.
Let me repeat the name of the Creator
A hundred thousand times on every turn.
This is the way to scale the stairs,
Climbing which one merges in the Lord.
Listening to the lofty tales of Celestial Beings,
The worm, too, started entertaining ambitions.
Says Nanak, it is His mercy alone that grants
    His audience,
The rest is the vain boast of the false. (32)

On my own I can neither speak nor remain silent.
On my own I can neither ask nor give.
On my own I can neither live nor die.
On my own I cannot be a ruler and get elated.
On my own I can neither gain Divine lore
    nor discuss it.
On my own I know not how to escape the world.
He whom He blesses wields power;
On one's own one is neither good nor bad. (33)

The Lord created nights and seasons,
Lunar days and week days,
Air and water, fire and the nether world,
Amidst these He installed the earth
To serve as an abode for meditation.
Therein He created living beings of various species.
And gave them ever so many names.
They do as they please;

The Lord remains True and His Court just,
Which is glorified by the elect,
Those whom His grace blesses.
The good and the bad will have to account for.
Says Nanak, their fate will be known on
*   arrival there.* (34)

The Dharam Khand is the realm of righteousness.
The Jnan Khand is the domain of knowledge
There are air, water and fire
Along with Krishnas and Shivas.
There are ever so many Brahmas
Creating colourful, charming figures in
*   various moulds.*
There are domains of activity and still mountains.
There are devotees seeking guidance.
There are deities and demons,
Silent sages and seas full of pearls.
There are mines (with precious stones) and
*   sweet tongues.*
There are several dynasties of sovereigns.
There is no end to the men of Divine Knowledge,
Nor to such servants of God.
Nanak has no count of them. (35)

In the Jnan Khand* the deliberations are daunting.
There are strains of music, singing
And rejoicing of untold varieties.
Beauty is the language of Shram Khand**

---

*   The realm of knowledge
** The realm of spiritual endeavour

There happen to be created unique figures.
Nobody can tell the tales of the place.
He who does so regrets it later.
Here spiritual awareness, intellect,
Understanding and enlightenment are shaped.
The evolved souls and men of miracles
Are rejuvenated here. (36)

There is spiritual love in the language of
    Karam Khand*
Except this there is nothing.
There are mighty heroes
Who are ever chanting Rama's Name,
Always absorbed in His adoration.
Their charm cannot be explained.
They never die nor can they be harmed,
Those in whose heart Rama abides.
The devotees of various realms dwell there.
With the True Lord in their heart, they make merry.
The Formless Lord dwells in the Sach Khand**
He beholds His creation in all His grace.
There are continents, solar systems and spheres.
If someone were to discuss them
There would be no end to it.
There are worlds after worlds
And creations after creations.
As He ordains so they do.
The Lord beholds, conjures and rejoices.

---

*   The realm of grace
** The realm of truth

Says Nanak, describing the World of Truth
is a hard task. (37)

Continence is the smithy,
Patience the goldsmith,
Understanding the anvil
And Divine knowledge the tool.
God's fear is the bellows
And penance the fire.
Love is the crucible
Where nectar is distilled.
The Lord's name is forged in this true mint.
Those who are favoured
Alone can do it.
Says Nanak, a graceful glance
Blesses and makes the devotee divine. (38)

Slok

Air is the Guru, water the father
And earth is the mother superior.
Day and night are the nursemaids
With whom the whole world plays.
Dharamraja sitting in the Lord's Court
Watches our deeds good and bad.
Depending upon our actions
We get close to or away from God.
Those who remember Him
Bear fruit.
Says Nanak, they've bright faces,
They ferry others along with them.

JAPUJI (1-8)

Sri Raga I Sector 3

Let good deeds be the soil and God's Word the seed;
Nourish it with truthful living.
Like a farmer cultivate faith in yourself
No need to bother about heaven or hell.

Don't be misled to believe
That He can be inveigled with mere words.
In the vanity of worldly love
And the pride of physical charm
You've frittered away this life.

Your body is like a slushy pond,
Your mind like a frog,
You've not cultivated acquaintance of the
      lotus flower.
The bumble-bee keeps reminding you like
      a teacher.
How can you understand, when you don't want
      to understand?

Those who are sold to lust for wealth,
Talking to them or their listening
Is like the blowing of the wind.
He who meditates on Him
Alone earns His grace.

You may fast for thirty days,
And say your prayers five times a day,
He who is called Satan may undo everything.
Says Nanak, you have to undertake a journey,
How come! you've collected all this luggage?

(23-24)

Sri Raga I Sector 2

Riches, youth and flowers are a few days' guests
Like the leaves of a weed that withers even in
    water.
You may enjoy life
As long as you are young and strong,
But your days are numbered; the body grows
    old and gets weary.
My loved ones have all gone to rest in
    the graveyard.
Afraid, I grieve in my faint voice
For one day I must also follow them.
Don't you hear the call, O fair one?
You must go to the in-laws;
No bride ever lives in her parents' home.
Says Nanak, the bride who lives in her parent's home
Is like the one whose house is burgled in
    broad daylight.
She loses her trousseau of virtues
And repairs loaded with sins.

(23)

Sri Raga I Sector 4

You are like an ocean, omniscient and
  omni-visioned!
I am a fish,
How can I measure You?
Wherever I turn, it is You I find;
The moment I get away, I die.
I know neither the fisherman nor the net.
In my moments of anxiety, I remember You.
You are here and there
And yet You appear far far away.
Whatever I do is within Your knowledge;
You know it all and yet I deny it.
Neither have I served You nor remembered You.
Whatever You offer I accept.
There is no other place where I can go.
My body and soul are dedicated to You.
You are close, You are far, You are in-between.
You see.
You hear.
You create the universe in Your image.
Says Nanak, whatever happens is ordained by You.
I must accept it.

(25)

Sri Raga I

In the unfathomable, brackish waters of the ocean
The fish noticed not the net,
Overconfident of her charm and wit
She fell into the trap and was caught.

Death can never be averted,
It hovers over your head.
In the manner of the fish
You'll be caught in this net unawares.

(55)

Sri Raga I

Wandering in the wilderness
I scale heights and go up the mountain.
I roam about in the jungle
But in the absence of a guide I do not find Him.
Without His Name I come and go.

I ask my fellow travellers
Who follow Him as slaves,
Deem Him as their Master
And walk into His house unquestioned,
How Do I enlist myself?

Says Nanak, the Lord prevails all over,
He has no second to lead to Him.

(57)

Sri Raga I

Everyone looks for pleasure
None for pain.
Those craving for pleasure
Are afflicted with severer pain.
The conceited seem not to understand this.
Those for whom weal and woe are alike

Have understood the secret
And attain bliss eternal.

(57)

Sri Raga I

Man! You should love God the way the
     lotus loves water.
Buffeted by waves, it still blossoms,
And longs for it.
Born in water, it withers without water.

Man! Without love there is no deliverance.
God dwells in you and blesses you with the
     gift of devotion.

Man! You should love God the way the fish
     loves water;
The more the water the happier she is.
Her heart and soul at peace,
She lives not a moment without water.
God alone knows the craving of her heart.

Man! Love God the way the pied cuckoo loves rain.
Not a drop of water it drinks
From the overflowing lakes and green pastures.
His grace alone grants him the raindrop;
His deeds avail him not.

Man! Love God the way water loves milk.
Mixed in milk, it evaporates
But does not allow the milk to scorch.
It's God who unites.

It's God who parts.
Only the truthful are blessed.
Man! Love God the way the shelduck loves the Sun.
She sleeps not for a moment
Lest she is distanced from her lover.
He who is conceited gains not His grace
The man of God lives in His company.

(59-60)

Sri Raga I

It's mere avarice
Your love for money and progeny, kinfolk and wife.
The world is misled by greed and ego,
Wealth and youthful charm.
My urge for attachment is my undoing.
The world, at large, is also afflicted with it.
Dear Lord! I have none other than You.
But for You I regard no one else.
That I am at peace with myself
It is at Your pleasure
It is Your guidance that makes me adore You.
I see no other count for it.
He who doesn't remember You falls a prey to pride.
Enlightenment is the gift of the Guru.
In its absence everything is poison.
Without good deeds, rich fare tastes insipid.
Born in avarice, it's avarice that kills with
     its caprice.
Evil deeds lead You to death;
It's Guru's Name that can save You.

SRI (61)

Sri Raga I

You may donate citadels of gold, horses and elephants,
You may donate land and comely cows,
You may still be petrified with pride.

You may be absorbed in His Name, a gift of the
        True Guru,
You may be an ascetic and a learned scholar
        of the Vedas,
You may yet be afflicted with entanglements
        of your mind.

A devotee alone can expect emancipation,
Everything else is beneath truth,
Above truth is truthful living.

(62)

Sri Raga I Sector 3

A recluse among recluses,
You indulge in pleasure amongst the pleasure-
        loving.
Nobody has been able to know You;
Neither in heaven, nor on earth, nor in the
        nether world.
I am sacrifice unto You and Your Name.
You have created this world
And made everyone an assignment.
You have thrown the dice and You watch the game.
You can be found in the world around.

Everyone longs for Your Name
Which can't be obtained without the True Guru.
The world is pitched in Maya.
I am sacrifice unto the True Guru,
A meeting with Him earns salvation.
He whom the angels and ascetics look for,
The True Guru has made me aware of Him.
I look for the holy men
In whose company I may remember His name.
My True Guru has made me understand
That remembering His Name is my only concern.

My Master has redeemed me
By placing both His hands on my head.
No other means did avail.
My Lord knows it all.
He has redeemed me with His manifest munificence.
Everyone has started hailing me.

He noticed not my good and bad deeds.
Living up to His reputation of a saviour
He endeared me to His heart,
And saved me from the blast of scorching winds.

(71-72)

Slok I

You may be a swan or a crane,
If it please Him
He may turn the swan into a crane.

(91)

Slok I

Good in words, I am bad in deeds.
Dirty in mind and comely in looks.
Emulating those who wait in attendance,
Devoted to the Lord, they enjoy His pleasant
*   company.*
Powerful and yet remaining powerless and
*   humble.*
Says Nanak, life would be worth living
If one came to associate oneself with the like of
*   them.*

(85)

Slok I

All gifts are His pleasure,
You may not argue with Him.
Those who are awake are ignored
And those asleep may be awakened and blessed.
The truthful have faith and contentment,
Also forbearance, the virtue of angels.
They are blessed with a glimpse of the Lord,
The guilty have nowhere to go.

(83)

Raga Majh

Slok I

He tells lies;
Which is like eating carrion,
And goes about preaching to others.
What a guide he is, says Nanak
Who is himself misled and beguiles others.

(140)

Slok I

If garments get soiled with blood stains,
How can they be pure in mind
Who suck the blood of humankind?
Says Nanak, remember God
With a wholesome heart and truthful tongue.
The rest is mere ostentation
With false deeds that we are wont to do.

(140)

Slok I

Let compassion be your mosque,
Devotion your prayer mat,

Truth and fairplay your Holy Qur'an.
Let your modesty be your circumcision
And courtesy your fast,
Your conduct be the Kaaba,
Rectitude your guide
And good deeds your creed and prayer.
The rosary should be what pleases Him.
Thus would He safeguard your honour.

(140-41)

Slok I

That which legitimately belongs to others
Is pork for him* there.
And beef for the one** here.
Your Guru or your pir will stand by you
Only if you don't eat what is forbidden.
Mere talking aloud doesn't reach you to heaven,
It's the truth that will obtain deliverance.
Just as dressing up the forbidden food
Doesn't make it permissible.
Says Nanak, false talk earns you nothing
*   but falsehood.*

(141)

Slok I

There are five prayers
To be said at five times.
All these five have their names.

---

*   The Muslim
** The Hindu

The first is truthfulness.
The second is honesty.
The third is charity in God's name.
The fourth is a clear mind and conscience.
And the fifth is singing His praises.
If these five form your conduct, you are a
*   real Muslim.*
Says Nanak, those who are false
Will lead others to falsehood.

                                                    (141)

Slok I

It is difficult to be a Muslim.
He who remains devoted in times of trial is a
Muslim.
He should first accept the Lord's faith
And shake off the false conceit.
Being the Prophet's Muslim means shedding the
*   fear of death*
And accepting the will of God.
With faith in the Creator, he is rid of the conceit.
And thus, if he is kind to all,
Says Nanak, he can be called a real Muslim.

                                                    (141)

Slok I

He alone lives whose heart is the abode of God,
Says Nanak, others live not.
If you live your life in humiliation,
All that you eat is like forbidden food.

The arrogance of authority, the pride in
  owning property,
Their naked and vulgar display,
Says Nanak, it is being cheated and beguiled.
Bereft of the name of God, one lives in ignominy.
It is no use eating,
It is no use dressing up,
If the True One doesn't dwell in your heart.
It's no use enjoying fruit,
It's no use relishing savoury and sweet dishes,
It's no use indulging in fine-ground flour-bread
  or meat.
Of no use are sheets on your comfortable bed
Where you revel in carnal pleasures.
It's no use commanding lashkars with mace-
bearers,
Arriving and residing in palaces.
Says Nanak, in the absence of the True Name
All the splendour is meaningless.

(142)

Slok I

Deep water is no worry for the fish,
Nor the vast sky for the bird.
How can the cold bother a stone?
Or family life a eunuch?
If (the essence of) sandalwood were to be applied
  to a dog
He would not change his nature.
Are the deaf to be enlightened

By the recitation of the Smritis to them?
No use providing light to the blind
By kindling even fifty candles.
You may offer gold to a cattle herd,
It would prefer eating grass.
Howsoever you may treat iron,
It will never turn into cotton.
Says Nanak, the identity of a fool is
That whatever he says, it leads to ruin.

(143)

Slok I

If bronze, gold or iron articles break,
The smith welds them with fire.
If the wife is estranged from the spouse,
The son brings them together.
Whatever the king demands,
Must be met and done right away.
The hungry is appeased
Only after he eats.
Relief from a dry spell comes
With rains and flooded streams.
Love is fostered with sweet words.
Truthfulness establishes a link with the Vedas.
The dead are remembered for good deeds.
Such are the bonds obtaining in this world,
The fool is silenced if smitten on the face.
It's Nanak's considered belief,
His adulation leads to His court.

(143)

Slok I

Tigers, hawks and the like carnivora
You make them eat grass.
And those who are grass-eating
You feed them on flesh.
You raise mounds in rivers
And turn deserts into fathomless oceans.
You bestow kingships on curs
And reduce lashkars to ashes.
Those who must breathe to live,
You make them live without breath.
Says Nanak, as it pleases the True One
He provides sustenance to His flock.

(144)

Slok I

Kaliyuga is a dagger,
Kings are butchers.
Dharma has taken wings and disappeared.
In the black night of falsehood
The moon of truth is nowhere to be seen.
I am lost in the search,
I find no way out of the darkness,
Afflicted with ego, I wail in sorrow,
Says Nanak, how do I attain deliverance?

(145)

Slok I

The rains satiate not the desert.
The hunger of the fire remains unappeased.
No king is content with his kingdom.

Who has ever assuaged the ocean?
Says Nanak, without the True Name
There is no end to one's search.

(148)

Slok I

Says Nanak, it is absurd
To ask for weal and not for woe.
Weal and woe are like garments
That a man must wear.
Where talking is of no avail,
It's better to remain quiet.

(149)

Pauri

If the True Guru is kind,
You get what you want.
If the True Guru is kind,
You never come to grief.
If the true Guru is kind,
No pain ever afflicts you.
If the true Guru is kind,
You enjoy every season.
If the True Guru is kind,
There is no fear of death.
If the True Guru is kind,
You live ever in peace.
If the True Guru is kind,
The nine treasures are yours.
If the True Guru is kind,
You merge with the Truth.

(149)

Raga Gauri

Gauri I

A compound of air, water and energy,
A plaything of capricious cerebration,
It has nine doors,
The tenth being the main entrance,
The learned must understand this.
He reveals, He speaks, it is He who listens.
He who reflects on himself, he alone knows Him.
It is the wind that whistles through the body
*   built of clay.*
Try to understand, O seer,
He is no other who is dead.
It is the vain consciousness and ego that die.
The omniscient never dies.
In search of whom you go to the holy shrines
That precious jewel you find in your mind.
The learned read and scan,
Indulge in meaningless controversies,
But know not the real Truth.
I don't die;
It is my accursed ignorance that expires.
He who is merged with the Omnipresent dies not.

Says Nanak, the Lord Guru has revealed to me,
For me, no one dies nor is born.

(152)

Gauri Cheti I

They are five and I am alone,
How do I guard my hearth and home?
They assail and assault me every day,
To whom shall I go and complain?
I must remember the Lord God
To enable me to face the fiends of doom.

Creating the shrine of the body with a door,
Within is installed the damsel soul.
Considering itself deathless, the body dissipates.
And they exploit it, his five evil mates.
The edifice is demolished and the shrine looted.
The lonely damsel is taken into custody.
When the bludgeon of death strikes
And shackles put around her neck,
All the five take to their heels.

The damsel looked for gold and silver
While her mates indulged in merry-making.
Says Nanak, those who commit misdeeds
Must be bound and taken to the town of death.

(155)

Gauri Cheti I

Who is the mother?
Who is the father?

Where have you come from?
What were you created for?
From fire and a drop of water?
My Lord! Who can count Your virtues?
I cannot recount my failures.

I've seen innumerable trees and plants.
Also the animals created by You.
So many serpents visited my hut
And many a bird I shooed away.

He breaks open shops
And ravages towns and temples.
Loaded with his loot he comes home
Looking around, right and left.
But how can he beguile you?

I have been to the banks of several rivers,
In the nine regions and in their shops
    and bazaars.
Like a trader I picked up a scale
And started weighing in my mind.
My sins are as many as the water-drops of
    an ocean.
Take pity on me, be merciful,
You have helped float sinking ships.
Something in me rages like a fire.
There is pain of a stab inside me.
Says Nanak, those who abide by His will
Are happy day and night.

(156)

Gauri Bairagan I

You've wasted your life
Sleeping at night and eating during the day.
It is the gem of a life
That you have lost for a shell.
You remembered not God.
O fool! You will repent for it ever after.
The night is gone in sleep and the day in eating,
The gem of a life is lost like a cowrie.
You have not remembered God,
Ignoramus! You will regret it.
He who keeps amassing untold wealth,
Knows not the Limitless,
Has no use for untold wealth.
If it could be got by one's own effort
Everyone would be prosperous.
You owe it to your karma
Not to your wishes.
Says Nanak, He takes care,
Who has created the world.
No one knows the ways of God,
And on whom and when He bestows His honour.

(156-57)

Gauri Bairagan I

Had I been a doe
I would live in a dale,
Eating leaves and grass
With the Guru's grace I would find my Lord.
I am a sacrifice unto Him!

I deal in His Name;
He is my goods-in-trade.

Had I been a koel
I would live in a mango tree,
Ever meditate on His Word.
And in due course meet my Lord,
He who is most charming to behold.

Had I been a fish
I would dwell in water
That sustains all life.
My Lord lives on this bank and that,
I would stretch my hand and gain His touch.

Had I been a snake,
I would live in a pit,
Absorbed in the Guru's Word
I would shed my fear.
Says Nanak, they are happily wedded
Who merge their flicker in His flame.

(157)

Gauri Guarevi I

It's God's grace that brings about the union.
His grace makes you virtuous.
His Word wipes away your sins.
The devotee gathers the wealth of His Name;
Without His Name it is a miserable life.
The stupid self-seeker amasses riches.
The devotee has Divine awareness bequeathed
by Karma.

The restless mind is wont to waver.
The True One does not relish untruth.
The devotee sings his Lord's praises.

(222)

Gauri I

It is His supreme will that prevails over all.
It is from Him that we all are created.
The paths may be two
But the Master is one.

(223)

Gauri I

A dissembler obsessed with ego knows not God.
Rare are the godmen wedded to the Lord.
The True One is not to be met with in arrogance.
To obtain the supreme seat, you must shed pride.
The ego of monarchs leads them to adventure.
They die in ego to be born again.
The Guru's Word helps rid arrogance;
Restraint of the mind kills evil passions.
The truth imbibed brings home in due course
Knowledge of the Master and secures the
*   supreme berth.*
A truthful living drives away the doubts of mind.
And assures an abode in the house of
*   the Fearless.*
Perishing in ego acquires no gain
He who adores the True Guru his conflicts
*   are resolved.*
Of little worth is what he sees

The awakened Guru-conscious sings His praises
And thus his bonds of ego are snapped
The devotee gains Divine knowledge and enjoys
*   eternal bliss.*

                                                    (226-27)

Gauri I

He who is imbued with the Lord's Name.
As the day dawns I long to have a glimpse of him.
It's your ill luck not to meditate on Him.
My Master is the provider for ever and ever.
The devotee who remembers my Lord, the Perfect,
The unstruck melody resounds in his mind.
He who likes meditating on His Name,
Is protected in all His mercy.
He in whose heart He abides,
Meeting him is untold bliss.
God lives in every living creature.
The conceited dies to be reborn in pride.
He understands God whom the Guru blesses;
He has his ego killed with the Guru's Word.
No more does he distinguish between the high
*   and the low.*
The devotee meets the Lord God with the grace
*   of the Guru.*
O Lord! Bless the worthless, the sinner in me,
It is by Your grace alone that I can be saved.

                                                    (228)

Gauri Poorbi Chhant I

The way the night of a bride in separation
Passes in sleeplessness,
The devotee grows frail
Suffering the pangs of separation.
The bride grows frail
Longing to have a glimpse of her groom.
No more interested in dressing herself up
Or enjoying dainty dishes,
Once proud of her youth and charm,
She is now like a squeezed out bust.
Says Nanak, the bride can meet her consort
Only when he so desires.
Without the groom her nights are sleepless.

(242)

Gauri Chhant I

Listen O my Lord God!
I am all alone in wilderness.
How can I have peace
Without meeting my Master however carefree
    He may be?
The bride cannot live without the groom.
Her nights become torturous agony;
Remembering You my love, I've lost my sleep.
Do listen to my entreaty.
Except you, who would take care of me?
I cry all alone in the wilderness.
Says Nanak, the bride suffers without the groom.
She meets Him only when He brings about
    the meeting.

(243)

Raga Asa

Asa I

He is called great on hearsay;
He alone who has seen Him can say how great
　　He is.
He can neither be described nor evaluated:
Those who have tried have failed.
O my Great Master, deep, profound and virtuous!
No one knows how great You are.
All the sages got together to meditate on You,
All the evaluaters got together to evaluate You,
The master thinkers and master divines
Could not measure a fraction of Your greatness!

(9)

Asa I

I remember You and I live,
I forget and I die.
It's not easy to remember You.
I hunger for Your Name;
Satisfying this hunger kills all pain.

Mother, how can I forget Him?
He is the True Lord, His Name is true.

Measuring a fraction of His greatness
Many have become wearied without success.
If everyone got together to do it,
He would neither be big nor small.
He never dies nor is He mourned.
He is always giving,
There is no end to His favours.
His measure is that there is none like Him.
Neither was one ever there,
Nor would there ever be another.
His gifts are as great as Him.
Those who pass their nights like days,
(They get to know Him.)
He is a wretch who forgets His Master.
Says Nanak, without His Name the mortal
    remains defiled.

(9-10)

Asa I

It is not the only sin I am soiled with
That I can wash away with virtue.
My spouse remains awake
And I sleep the night through.
How can I endear myself to Him
Who is awake while I slumber?
Swarming with longing I go to His bed,
I know not if I would be accepted.
I wonder what is in store for me,
Without seeing Him I cannot live.
Having not had a sip of His love,
My thirst remains ever unquenched.

When her youth is gone, the damsel regrets;
Lovelorn she may now keep awake,
She has only sorrow and regret to share.
Shedding her ego if she were to do herself up,
Maybe she'd enjoy the bed of her love.
Says Nanak, she endears herself to the spouse,
Who forgets herself and surrenders to the Lord.

(356-57)

Asa I

I remained utterly ignorant at my parents' home,
I knew nothing about my love.
My Master is like none else.
It's His grace that I met Him.
At the in-laws' I perceived the truth
And thereby came to understand Him.
It's Guru's grace that confers wisdom,
How could one please one's spouse?
Says Nanak, she who adorns herself with fear and love,
She enjoys His bed for ever and ever.

(357)

Asa I

There are six houses, six teachers and
        six sermons.
However, the teacher of teachers remains the same.
The house where the Creator is adored,
Let me, with Your grace, belong to it.
There are seconds and minutes, hours and periods,
Lunar days, week days and months.

However, the Sun remains the same;
The seasons may be many.
Says Nanak, all these are my Lord's varied revelations.

(357)

Asa I Sector 6

Let the mind be the jewel
And the breath the thread that links,
If the damsel were to weave it with humility,
She would enjoy her Lord's company.

Lord! I am fascinated by Your manifold virtues.
None else can match Your splendour.

If she were to wear the necklace of His Name,
Dazzling like her teeth,
And if her bracelet were her good deeds,
She would be able to endear herself to Him.

If her finger-ring were the slayer of Madh*
And Godly her silken dress,
Patience woven into her plaited hair,
And excellence the kohl in her eyes,
Her heart, the light, and her body, the bed,
When such a realisation comes to her,
She will consummate her wedding.

(359)

---

*   Evil

Asa I

Let knowledge be the molasses,
Meditation, the mahua flowers
And good luck the fermenting agent,
With faith as the furnace
And love the cover,
This is how the Divine Nectar is distilled.
Man! If the seeker were to sip this nectar of
      His Name
He would merge in the Lord God.
He would remain lost in Divine love,
      day and night
And enjoy the unstruck melody.
The Perfect One will then bless him with the
      cup of truth,
The cup He offers to those He takes kindly to.
He who deals in nectar does not dabble in
      spurious drinks.
The Guru's Word is the Divine decree,
He who imbibes it becomes acceptable.
He who is privileged to visit His Court,
He cares not for salvation or heaven.
He who is imbued with His adoration,
He is an eternal anchorite.
In the gamble of life he loses not.
Listen O Bharthrahari Yogi!
Nanak is inebriated with this nectar.

(360)

Asa I

He occupied Khurasan and subdued Hindustan.
God! don't You blame Yourself for having sent the
    Mughal like a doom?
Seeing such suffering and wailing,
Didn't it hurt You O Lord?
You are the lone Creator of us all.
If an aggressor were to kill an aggressor,
I wouldn't complain.
But when a fierce lion falls on a herd of innocent
    cattle,
The Master must take the blame.
The dogs have ruined the gem of my country,
When they die, none will ever mourn them.
O God, You alone make and unmake, this is
    Your greatness.
If anyone else were to style himself as great
And indulge in pleasure-seeking,
He would be like a worm in Your eyes,
Feeding on a few grains.
He who dies in life, says Nanak,
Lives by meditating on the Name of God.

(360)

Slok I

It is in the Lord's fear that the wind blows.
It is in His fear that rivers flow.
It is in His fear that fire functions perforce.
It is in His fear that the earth remains burdened.
It is in His fear that Indra flies headlong.

It is in His fear that the Dharmraja waits at
    His door.
The Sun and the Moon fear Him,
They move about millions of miles without end.
The ascetics, sages and savants live in His fear.
The span of the sky is stretched in His fear.
It is in His fear that multitudes of warriors
And heroes full of glory come and go.
Everyone lives in His fear destined for him.
Says Nanak, it is the Formless alone who fears
    Him not.

(464)

Slok I

Divine understanding is attained not through talk.
It is a difficult task indeed.
It's Your Karma that helps you gain it.
All the rest is vain endeavour.

(465)

Slok I

You may read and read and load yourself like a cart.
You may read and read and equip yourself fully.
You may read and read and commit yourself.
You may read and read and dig pits around you.
You may read for years.
You may read for months and months.
You may read as long as you live.
You may read as long as you breathe.

*Says Nanak, only one thing will be reckoned in
    the end,*
The rest is all vanity and vexation.

(467)

Slok I

You will be truthful if you are true at heart;
*With the filth of falsehood washed away, your body
    is clean and pure.*
You will be truthful if you love the True One;
Hearing His Name you will be ecstatic
And arrive at the threshold of salvation.
*You will be truthful if you are aware of the true
    way of life;*
*Treating this body as the seed-bed, you sow
    His Name in it.*
You are truthful if you follow true advice;
A heart full of compassion, you take to giving charity.
*You are truthful if you live in the sanctum of
    your soul,*
Taking instructions from the Guru, you abide by them.
Truth is the remedy which washes away the sins.
Nanak is the supplicant to those who are truthful.

(468)

Slok I

Suffering is the remedy; comfort the malady,
Where there is comfort, You are not there.
You are the Creator, I dare not do anything.

Even if I tried, I may not succeed.
I am sacrifice unto You whom I behold
  in Nature.
Your extent can't be known.
You are in the universe like light;
The light that enlightens.
You prevail all over.
You are the true, praiseworthy Lord.
He who adores You finds salvation.
Says Nanak, the Creator has His own ways,
He does what He pleases.

(469)

Slok I

A man of Dharma
Wastes his life lived in Dharma
Asking for heaven (as his reward.)

(469)

Slok I

Says Nanak, the world is a chariot
And it has a charioteer.
It keeps changing, age after age.
The devotees understand it best.
The Satyayug was the age of contentment,
It had Dharma *as its charioteer.*
The Tretayug was the age of continence,
It had prowess as its charioteer.
The Dwaparyug was the age of penance,
With truth as its charioteer.

The Kaliyug is the age of fire,
With flasehood as its charioteer.

(470)

• • •

Slok I

In Kaliyug, Atharva is the Veda
And God's name is Allah!
You wear the blue garments
And live the way the Turks and Pathans do.

(470)

• • •

Says Nanak, a sweet tongue is the essence
of all virtue.

(470)

• • •

They perform puja and read the Qur'an on
the quiet;
But in the open they have adopted the ways
of the Turks.

(471)

• • •

Says Nanak, only he would be welcome there
Who works hard, earns and shares with others.

(472)

• • •

Eating and drinking is a sacred act;
.The bounties are given to be enjoyed.

(472)

• • •

Why decry her who raises the rajas?

(473)

• • •

He who is born must die;
Everyone has to take his turn.

(474)

• • •

You have to solve your problems
With your own devices.

(474)

• • •

He makes vessels Himself,
He fills them Himself.
Some contain milk,

Others are hauled onto the fire.
Some have a peaceful sleep,
Others keep a vigil,
Says Nanak, blessed are they
To whom He takes kindly.

(475)

Raga Bihagda

Slok I

Demons have come to be born in the Kaliyug;
Sons are demons, demons are daughters,
Their mothers are the chief demons.

The Hindus are misled;
They have forgotten the Primal Lord.
As stated by Narad
They have taken to worshipping idols.
They are blind and deaf, stone-blind indeed.
Uneducated, simpletons, they pick up stones
*   and adore them;*
How on earth can stones that themselves drown,
Cruise them across?

(556)

Raga Wadhans

Wadhans I Sector 2

The peahen sings.
It is the rainy season.
I feel a stab in my heart.
Your charm is irresistible.
I will die if I see You not.
I am sacrifice unto You!
When You are mine, I feel proud.
Without You what for should I be vain?
I saw You in my dream
But You disappeared.
I cry, my eyes swimming in tears.
Lord! I cannot come to You,
Nor can I send anyone,
Let me sleep again,
Maybe I would see my Master.
Says Nanak, what should I offer him
Who comes and gives me tidings of my Lord?
I offer him my beheaded head for a seat
And I serve him without my head.
Why should one not die and lay down one's life
If one's Lord is found estranged?

(557-58)

Slok I

Forget the ceremonial
That makes you forget the Lord.

Pauri

Says Nanak, that relation is welcome
Which endears you to the Master.

The bride is at home,
The groom is away,
She misses him and pines for him.

If the mindset is right
It should take not long
For a meeting with the Lord.

(590)

Raga Sorath

Sarath I Sector I

Let your mind be the peasant that does the farming,
Hard work be the water and your body the field.
Let His Name be the seed and contentment
    the cover.
And don the dress of humility.
Then alone will love be born with His favour.
Such a one is blessed...
If you arrived in God's kingdom like this
You would find a place in the palace of bliss.
Let the service you take be devotion
And God's Name the striving.

Let your labour be eschewing evil deeds.
Only then will people commend you.
Says Nanak, if He were to be gracious,
Man must flourish in life manifold.

(595-96)

Sarath I

I am a foul sinner, an inveterate dissembler,
You are pure, blemishless God.

Those who come under Your care
Taste nectar and are drunk with eternal bliss.
God! You are the pride of the humble,
Those who are given to remembering You
Are proud possessors of Your Name,
You are perfect; I am puny and mean.
You are great; I am petty.
I remember You day and night.
My tongue utters Your Name time and again.
You are Truthful, I am devoted to You.
Understanding the mystery of Your Word
I have realised the secret of truth.
They are truthful who remember you day and night.
Those who are false are born, and they die.
There is none other whom I may adore.

There is none who can equal You.
Nanak is the slave of Your slaves.
It's by dint of the Guru's Word that
    I've known the Lord

(596-97)

Sorath I Sector I

You are the Bountiful Lord
Given to proffering doles.
I am only a beggar,
What should I ask for?
There is nothing that would last.
Grant me the longing for Your Name.
You dwell in every heart,

You sustain the earth, the ocean and the sky.
It's God's Name that makes one have Your glimpse.
With His grace my True Lord
Has revealed Himself on the earth, in the nether
*   world and the sky.*
My Lord is beyond birth.
He is there, He will be there.
I peeped into my heart
And had a glimpse of Him.
The wily world is caught in the cycle of
*   birth and death.*
It makes one forget His Name.
It's only when one meets the True Guru
That one gains understanding.
The non-believer loses this game.
The True Guru has unshackled and set me free.
I am not going to be born again.
Nanak has gained the jewel of Divine awareness,
He is merged in the Formless One.

(597-98)

Sorath Sector 3

I sing as it pleases Him
And thus I reap the fruit.
I reap the fruit
If He so desires.
My Guru has granted me the treasure of
*   His Name*
And I am thereby merged in Truth.
As I understand the Guru's Word

I shed the worldly wit.
The light of the Guru's Word
Has dispelled the darkness around.
As I meditate on the Guru's feet
I quit the path of death.
In His fear I have found the Fearless.
This is how I arrived at my Lord-of-No-Haste.
Says Nanak, after careful thought,
It is deeds only that matter in the world.
Good deeds are His adoration,
This is how He is met.

(599)

Sorath I Sector I

Those who have savoured it,
They alone know its taste;
The dumb eating a delicacy,
Cannot describe the indescribable.
Do as He wishes you to do.

(635)

Raga Dhanansri

Dhanasri I

Says Nanak, as long as you live in this world,
Speak out your heart, you may;
And listen to what others have to say.

(661)

Dhanasri I

If He is kindly disposed,
It makes you remember Him.
The soul softens and gets attuned.
He who identifies himself with the Supreme
Suffers not from duality.
God is attained through the Guru's grace.
Death doesn't devour
Those who meditate on Him.
Following the true path leads to enlightenment.
One remains untainted even amidst stark evil.
One finds emancipation living with the spouse and sons,
Such is the greatness of God.
One should serve the Lord, the way
One submits oneself to Him to whom
    one belongs.

123

One should accept what is acceptable to the Lord.
Such a slave is welcome in His Court.
He who enshrines the True God's name in his
  heart,
Attains whatever he asks for.
He to whom the True Lord is kind,
Need have no fear of death.
Says Nanak after much thought,
He who remembers the True Word,
Attains salvation.
The Guru's Word is the essence of all spiritual striving.

(661)

Dhanasri I

It avails not talking too much,
You are known well enough without it.

(661)

Dhanasri I Arati

The sky is the platter,
The Sun and the Moon are lights,
And the stars jewels.
The sandalwood's fragrance is the incense,
The wind is the flywhisk
And all the forests Your flowers.
What a wonderful arati it is!
Oh, You destroyer of life and death!
The melody of Your Name is an unending strain.
You have a thousand eyes and yet not one eye.
You have a thousand forms and yet not one form.

You have a thousand unsoiled feet and yet
    not one unsoiled foot.
You have a thousand noses and yet not one nose.
Your ways have left me charmed, O Lord!
There is my Lord's light which enlightens everyone.
By the Guru's grace the truth becomes manifest.
This arati is what pleases my Lord.
I hunger for the fragrance of Your lotus feet
    day and night.
O Lord! Grant a drop of water of Your grace
To Nanak the thirsty bird,
So that he finds solace in Your Name.

(663)

Dhanasri I Sector 2

The Guru is like an ocean laden with pearls.
The swans of saints sitting on its shore peck
    at the pearls.
They partake of the elixir of His Name if He so pleases,
And thus they meet their Creator in the ocean
    itself.
The wretched crane bathes in the puddle;
Rather than cleaning itself, it acquires filth.
The wise take every step with care;
Shedding duality, they are devoted to the Formless.
Repeating His Name they attain salvation
And are freed from the cycle of birth and death.
A swan never leaves the ocean.
He merges with the Lord with devotion and love.
The swan is in the ocean and the ocean in the swan,
It's an untold tale revealed by the grace of the Guru

(685)

Raga Tilang

Tilang I Sector I

I wish to make a submission, my Lord!
If You would please lend me Your ear.
You are a truly great, merciful and faultless Sustainer.
That this world is not long-lasting,
I am convinced.
That the messenger of death would catch hold of
  me by my hair
I am well aware.
Wife, son, father and brother,
None would be able to hold my hand.
In the end, when I fall and it is my time to depart
None would come to my rescue.
I roam about daily, given to avarice and evil ways
Never do I do a good deed.
Such a wretched one I am;
Ill-omened, miserly, careless, narrow-minded and
rude.
Says Nanak, but I am Your slave,
The dust of the feet of Your servants.

(721)

Tilang I Sector 3

This body is lost completely to Maya;
It's dyed in avarice.
My Lord doesn't like such garments.
How may I go to His bed?
I am sacrifice unto Him,
I am sacrifice unto Him,
I am sacrifice unto Him who remembers Your
    Name.
He who remembers Your Name,
I am sacrifice unto him a thousand times.
Let your body be the container,
Put the fast colour of His Name in it
And let the great Dyer dye it.
No one has known such a colour!
The Lord is with them
Who are garbed in red.
Nanak craves for the dust of their feet.
He creates, He dyes, He blesses.
Says Nanak, she who is acceptable to the Master
He makes her remember His name.

(721-22)

Tilang I

The newly-wed! Why do you throw your
    weight about?
Why don't you enjoy the company of your Groom
    at home?
Stupid! Your Spouse is close at hand,
Why must you go out looking for Him?

With the kohl of fear in your eyes,
Dress yourself in the garments of devotion,
You will then be called a bride
And your spouse will deign to endear you to him.

What should the newly-wed do
If she doesn't find favour with the spouse?
She implores Him time and again
But she doesn't get access to the Master's mansion.
She must do whatever He likes,
Without good deeds nothing can be had.
You may try as much as you may,
Given to avarice, greed and ego
And thus sold to Maya,
The newly-wed should understand
One doesn't gain the Master's pleasure.

She should go and ask the one with fond Spouse:
How does one gain the groom's favour?
Do whatever He asks you to do
And give up being clever and demanding.
He who bestows on you the treasure of love
You must be devoted to Him.
Apply the perfume of doing what he commands
And surrender to Him in body and soul.
So says the happily married,
This is how you gain the Master's favour.

You have to lose yourself to gain His favour,
There is no other way.
The day the Master looks kindly upon you,

It is a fruitful day indeed,
It's like acquiring Nine Treasures.
She is a blessed one who is fond of her Spouse.
She is the queen, says Nanak.

Dyed in such a colour, lost in devotion,
Drowned in His love day and night,
She is comely, charming, personable and wise.

(722)

Raga Suhi

Suhi I Sector 2

He abides within you,
Not anywhere outside.
Instead of the nectar
Why must you sip poison?
You should gain the awareness
That makes you follow the True Lord.
Everyone talks about knowledge and devotion
And yet the world remains shackled.
He who serves his fellows follows the Lord,
The Lord who pervades the earth and ocean.
I am not good nor is anyone bad.
Nanak prays to God Who alone can save.

(728)

Suhi I

The vessel is good if He likes it.
A much dirtied vessel
Can't be cleaned by mere washing.
It's the Guru's temple that imparts true knowledge,
A place which washes clean.
It's He who makes you distinguish between good
*   and bad;*

Let no one assume that he can do it on his own.
You are moulded according to your deeds,
His Name is the nectar
And He alone offers it,
After which you depart with honour and glory
With trumpets playing for you.
Not only the poor people,
The three worlds would sing your praises.
Says Nanak, such a one would be blessed
And would liberate all his people.

(729-30)

Suhi I

What scale, what measure, who should be the evaluator?
Which Guru should guide me?
How should I determine Your status?
My Precious One! You are beyond my reckoning.
You are all over;
In water and on earth,
In everything living.
Let my mind be the scale, my heart the measure,
And Your service my evaluator.
Let me reckon You in the heart of my hearts.
This is how I would like to go about it.
You are the scale, You are the measure,
    You are the evaluator.
You watch Yourself, You assess Yourself, You are
    the trader.
Nanak lives in the company of the blind,
The petty,
Those who know You not.

He remains restless,
How can one so stupid get close to You?

(730-31)

Suhi I Chhant, Sector 2

My Beloved has come to my house.
He has come on His own.
My wait has endeared me to Him.
Having met Him, I am at peace.
I've got what I longed for.
Now I am by His side, day and night.
I am happy in my heart.
My house, a temple, is enchanting,
There is an ever-resounding symphonic melody
      of five notes.
My Lord has come to my house.

(764)

Suhi I Sector 3

Come, my Loved One, I crave for You.
Excited, I await You at my threshold.
O Lord! listen to my prayer
I long to see You.
You are my support;
A glimpse and I am liberated,
Freed from the agony of life and death.
I see Your light in every living thing;
You can be seen only when You enlighten.
Nanak is sacrifice unto his Lord.
Meeting whom is living a truthful life.

(764-65)

Suhi I Chhant, Sector 4

If you have the musk of virtues,
The fragrance will be secreted.
If such virtues are obtained from a friend,
These may also be shared.
Share only the virtues,
Eschewing the vices.
Dressed in silk with elaborate make up
You may assume the centre of stage in life.
Wherever you go, do sing His praises,
Skimming nectar with every phrase.
If you have a musk of virtues,
The fragrance will be secreted.

(765-66)

Suhi I

If you lose the sense of belonging
You become alien in your own country.
Whom shall I take into confidence?
My heart is crowded with woes,
The whole world is in agony,
Who will come to take care of me?
It is dreadful, this coming and going,
There is no end to the cycle.
Without Guru's Name, man is small and petty,
If you heed not the Guru's Word,
You lose the sense of belonging;
You become alien in your own country.

(766)

Slok I

Even when the nights are dark
White remains white.
When the bright day is scorching hot
Black remains black.
The blind, without discretion,
Remain ignorant and stupid.
Says Nanak, in the absence of His grace
They can never gain respectability.

(789)

Slok I

He who has not tasted the elixir of love
And the affection of the spouse,
Is like the guest of a deserted house,
Who, as he comes, goes away unattended.

(790)

Raga Bilawal

Bilawal I

You are called the Sultan, my Master!
You are beyond my praise.
I have what You give,
A simpleton, I know not what to ask for.
Grant me the understanding that I sing
    Your praises
And I live a truthful life, as ordained by You.
Whatever happens is under Your command.
You are known everywhere.
O Master! I know not Your limits.
What virtues can a blind man possess?
How can I sing Your praises,
Sing them and measure You?
I cannot sing,
I am incapable of it,
Whatever You say, I repeat the same.
It's no adoration indeed!
There are ever so many seekers,
I am a novice among them,
Asking for myself alone.
But if I am devoid of devotion

I'll bring a bad name to Him
Whose slave I am.

(795)

Bilawal I Score I

My mind is a temple.
Dressed like a dervish
I bathe in my heart.
My only cherished desire is
Not to be born again.
I am devoted to my benevolent Lord.
He knows not my heart's ache
As I care not for other's agony.
O my Inaccessible, Incomprehensible,
Invisible and Infinite Master!
Pray, take care of me.
You pervade the sea, land and the sky,
Every soul has Your spark.
My learning, wisdom and understanding are
   Your gifts.
My mansions and monasteries are Yours.
My Lord! I know none other than You.
I sing Your praises every day.
All living beings look up to You.
Their well-being is Your concern.
Whatever pleases You, O Lord, is welcome.
This alone is Nanak's supplication.

(795)

Bilawal I

You are the Word
And the Symbol.
You hear Yourself
And then acquire knowledge.
You create the world
And watch its expanse.
You are my benign Lord.
Your Name is the sanction,
Your Name is without blemish.
I am a beggar,
You are my Invisible, Inscrutable Master.
The love of Maya is like loving an evil woman.
Unseemly, adulteress, witch.
False is worldly power or good looks,
Lasting just for four days.
Your Name can turn darkness into light.
I have tried and discarded Maya.
I have no doubt about it.
He whose father is alive,
Cannot be called illegitimate.
He who is devoted to the Lord
Fears none.
The Creator creates and makes others join Him.
He who is disciplined by the Word
Alone can control his mind.
He stays at rest and is devoted to the Lord True.
He who is sacrifice unto God,
Nothing else ever occurs to him.
Says Nanak, those who imbibe Your Name
They are emancipated.

(795-96)

Raga Ramkali

Ramkali I, Sector 1

Some study the Vedas.
Others read the Puranas.
Some meditate on You with rosaries,
I know not this or that.
I remember just Your Name.
I know not my Lord what is in store for me.
Stupid and ignorant, I come seeking refuge in you.
At times I soar high in the skies,
At others I touch the nadir.
Greedy that I am, my mind is never steady,
It goes about probing the four corners of
    the world.
I came to the world destined to die,
And yet I amassed wealth for a long long life.
I see people go,
I also see the fire travelling towards me.
Neither friend nor brother,
Neither father nor mother;
Says Nanak, if the Lord were to take charge
    of you,
He would certainly take care of you.

(876)

Ramkali I

Says Nanak, listen O Machhandir!
He who disciplines the five demons,
Never wavers.
He who is used to this yoga,
Saves himself along with his family.
He alone is a recluse who is realised;
He remains submerged in a serene trance.
With a beggar's bowl he asks for God's love,
Lives in fear,
And is thus sated with the priceless gift of
*   contentment.*
He becomes an image of meditation.
He is sacrifice unto God.
He is an adept, an ascetic, a Yogi and a mendicant,
He who meditates on the Lord God.
They who anoint the Guru's feet,
Attain realisation of the Word.
I practise neither Japu nor am I a penitent,
I am not disciplined, nor do I perform any rituals.
I just utter His Name.
Nanak has worshipped his Guru, the Lord God
And realised Him through the True Word.

(877)

Ramkali I

Of what avail is
Worship without self-respect?
Discipline without righteousness?
The sacred thread without self-denial?

You may bathe and wash,
You may put on the sacrificial mark,
But without truth you remain misled.

In the Kaliyug only the Qur'an is accepted.
The Brahmin and his sacred works are discarded.
Even Nanak is known as Rahman!

God! You are the Creator,
You know it all best!

(903)

Ramkali I

Undertaking ascetic practices is wasting
    one's body.
Fasting and penance soften not the soul.
No worship can compare with remembering God.

Man! Serve your Guru and seek the company
    of godmen.
Sip the elixir of His Name
Neither the demon of death
Nor the serpent of Maya *will dare assail you.*

(905)

Ramkali I

It is the Divine will that Brahma came into being.
It is the Divine will that he was bestowed
    perception
It is the Divine will that eternity and the ages
    were created.

*It is the Divine will that the Vedas
    were produced.
It is the Divine will that the Word, the Saviour,
    descended.
It is the Divine will that the God-conscious are
    emancipated.
The Word-Divine should be carefully listened to.
The Word-Divine is the essence of the
    three worlds.
Listen O scribe! Of what use are these
    entanglements?
You should write the Divine Name alone,
The Cherisher of the world.*

(929-30)

Ramkali I

*The crow is again caught in the net;
He regrets it but it's too late.
Even trapped, he pecks at the feed
But tries not to understand.
Only if he meets the true Guru
Will his eyes open.*

*Like a fish you are caught in a death-trap
Without the help of the benevolent Guru
There is no deliverance,
You come and go again and again.
Dyed in fast colour
You remain absorbed in Him.
Emancipated this way
You never get caught in the trap again.*

(935)

Sidh Gosht
(Guru Nanak's dialogue with miracle-makers)

There is but one God. He is realised through the
grace of the True Guru.

The Siddhas sat in an assembly,
A venerable gathering of godmen!

I salute the Truthful and the Exalted!
I would slice my head
And offer it to Him with my body and soul.
Says Nanak, it is in the company of saints
That one realises the truth
Which leads to glory sublime.
It's no use roaming about.
It is the truth alone that purifies;
Without the True Word
There is no salvation. (1)

"Who are you?
What is your name?
What course have you adopted?
For what purpose?
Tell us the truth.

This is what we pray for.
We are sacrifice unto the saints!
Where is your seat?
Where do you belong?
Whence do you come?" (2)

Says Nanak:
Listen O ascetics!
Do you wish to know which path I follow?
My seat is in my heart
Where I constantly live.
I walk the path He traces out for me.
I adopt the course directed by Him.
I live as He pleases.
I sit in meditation on the Eternal Lord
As initiated by the Guru.
Those who are God-conscious realise
That He bestows the perception
And one merges into the Truthful. (3)

"The world is a virtual hazardous ocean
How does one cross it?"
Asks Charpat, "O Nanak, the recluse!
Tell us the secret." (4)

Says Nanak:
He who asks the question understands better,
What reply can one give him?
The way a lotus lives in water unfringed,
Or a duck swims against the current,
One should meditate on the Divine Word.

This is the way to cruise across the dreaded
    ocean;
One should opt for loneliness
And concentrate on the Absolute.
Cherishing hope even in hopelessness,
He sees and makes others see
The inaccessible and the incomprehensible.
Nanak is the slave of such a One. (5)

"Listen O Master!
It is our prayer,
We wish to know the truth,
Don't take offence.
Pray, tell us, how can one gain access to the
    Guru's gate?"

Says Nanak:
With Name as support
The restless mind finds abode in the House
    of Truth
When one takes to truth
The Creator brings about the union. (6)

Said the Yogis, continuing their plea:
"We have quit our business and our status,
We live under trees and in woods in the jungle,
Roots and fruits form our food,
We go and bathe at the places of pilgrimage,
And thereby remain contented
Without contracting any sins!"

Observes Loharipa, the Deputy of Gorakh,
"This is our way of seeking union with God." (7)

Says Nanak:
You may live at home or anywhere else,
You continue to covet others.
Without His Name your mind is not at peace.
And your hunger is not satisfied.
My Guru has created the shop and the
*   shopping-centre within me*
I trade here in truth, in His grace sublime.
I sleep and eat little,
This is the essence of my creed. (8)

You wear the garb of a Yogi
With earrings, a beggar's bowl and
*   patched garbs.*
Out of the six schools of philosophy
Adopt one and follow it inside and out.
This is the way to harness the mind
So that you fault not again. (9)

The Guru-conscious understand it as the
*   essential* Yoga:
The Divine Word, enshrined within you.
Your earrings should be shedding ego
*   and attachment.*
Forsaking lust, anger, conceit,
Inculcate understanding of the Guru's teachings.
If these are your begging bowl and
*   patched-up garb*

And you see God everywhere
The Lord will cruise you across.
He is True; His Name is Truthful.
My Guru has testified to this. (10)

Your beggar's bowl should be detachment from
    the world.
And the five elements your head-gear.
Your body should be the prayer-mat
And the loin-cloth your mind.
Truth, contentment and self-discipline be your
    companions.
Thus you become God-conscious and you meditate
    on His Name. (11)

"Who is the unmanifest?
Who is liberated?
Who is the link between what is inside and
    what is outside?
Who comes and who goes?
Who it is who pervades the three worlds?" (12)

Says Nanak:
He pervades each and every heart.
Those devoted to the Guru are emancipated.
It is the Divine Word which links
That who is within and the one without.
Those who are conceited die;
They come and go.
The Guru-conscious remain tuned to the Truthful. (13)

*"How is one caught and devoured by the serpent
   of evil?
How does one lose?
How does one gain?
How does one remain pure?
How does one dispel darkness?
We shall take as our Guru
One who can reveal this secret."* (14)

*Says Nanak:
The misled gets caught
And is devoured by the serpent of evil.
The conceited loses,
The Guru-conscious gains.
Meeting the True Guru dispels darkness.
When one is rid of ego, one merges in the Lord.* (15)

*He who is tied to the infinite
Doesn't collapse like a wall;
His soul doesn't fly off like a swan.
The cave of bliss becomes his permanent abode.
The True Lord loves the truthful.* (16)

*"What for have you renunciated your home?
What for have you adopted the garb of
   a recluse?
What are the wares you trade in?
How will you cruise across?"* (17)

*Says Nanak:
I became a recluse in search of the
   Guru-conscious.*

It is to have a glimpse of the Lord
That I have adopted this garb.
I trade in truth alone,
I shall cruise across with the Guru's grace. (18)

"How have you changed the course of your life?
Who is it you are attached to?
How have you curbed your dreams and desires?
With what device did you kindle the light within?
How can one eat* iron without teeth?
O Nanak! Acquaint us with the truth." (19)

Says Nanak:
Born with the True Guru's blessings
I've changed the course of my life;
I've attuned my mind to the celestial symphony.
I've set fire to all my hopes and desires.
With the grace of the Guru, I found the light
within me.
I undid the** three states of mind
And I ate iron without teeth.
It's only the Saviour who saves. (20)

"As regards the beginning,
What do you think?
Which sphere of the void did He dwell in?
What is the earring of knowledge?
Who is it that lives in everyone's heart?
How can one escape the blow of death?

---

*   Encounter evil
** Raj Guna, Tam Guna & Satya Guna

And how does one go to the house of the Fearless?
How does one become steady occupying the seat
of contentment?
And annihilate one's adversaries?"

Says Nanak:
With Guru's Divine Word, the evil of ego
is undone;
One gains admission into His abode.
He who has brought about Creation
Nanak knows Him by His Divine Word
And remains His slave. (21)

"Where does one come from?
Where does one go?
Where does one terminate?
How does one understand the truth of the Formless
And get devoted to Him?
He is the Judge, He is the petitioner too,
Nanak! Do throw light on this."

Says Nanak:
Man comes as ordained by Him,
He goes under His command.
As He pleases he abides by Him,
He leads a truthful life under the Absolute Guru
And the Word-Divine makes him realise God's
grandeur and excellence. (22)

One can only wonder about the Primordial.
The Lord lived in His own void.

Desirelessness is the earring of the
    Guru's knowledge
Which lives in my heart.
You get merged in the Fearless One
By the grace of the Guru's Word
And get identified with Pure Reality.
Says Nanak, he who serves none other
Succeeds in his search.
He understands the wondrous command,
And the truth of life and its being,
With truth enshrined in his heart.
He who denies himself and remains detached
Can be called a true ascetic. (23)

From formlessness the Lord assumed an
    immaculate form,
From attributelessness He acquired attributes.
With the grace of the True Guru
One attains the supreme status
And gets merged into the True Name.
He then recognizes the True Lord
And gets rid of ego and arrogance.
He is the Yogi who imbibes the Guru's Word.
The lotus of knowledge blossoms in his heart.
He who kills his conceit
Becomes omniscient
And understands the All-Merciful.

Says Nanak:
He is honoured
Who endears himself to everyone around him. (24)

Emerged from Truth, he merges into Truth,
And becomes identified with the Truthful.
The false ones arrive;
Finding no place, they come and go.
It is the Divine Word that helps
escape transmigration.
He Himself assesses and grants pardon.
He who is afflicted with duality
Forgets the alchemy of Name.
He alone understands whom He makes
understand.
The Guru's Word bestows emancipation.
Says Nanak, It is only the Boatman who can
ferry across
Those who are rid of ego and duality. (25)

The conceited are misled;
They are destined for death.
They envy others and suffer loss after loss.
The egoist given to doubting wanders about
in wilderness.
He who recites incantations in the
cremation ground,
Is misled.
He understands not the Divine Word
And utters foul phrases.
Says Nanak, those devoted to Truth
Live a peaceful life. (26)

The Guru's devotee fears the Truthful.
The Guru's Devotee is soft-spoken.

The Guru's devotee sings adulatory praises.
The Guru's devotee attains unimpeachable
  super-status.
The Guru's devotee breathes in His Name with
  every pore of his body.
Says Nanak, the Guru's devotee merges in the Truth. (27)

The Guru's devotee is preoccupied with the study
  of the Vedas.
The Guru's devotee is preoccupied devising means
  to swim across.
The Guru's devotee is preoccupied
  with understanding the Divine Word.
The Guru's devotee is preoccupied with
  the mysteries of the Interior.
The Guru's devotee imbibes the Invisible and
  the Infinite.
Says Nanak, the Guru's devotee arrives close
  to emancipation. (28)

The Guru's devotee gets to know unrevealed
  thoughts.
The Guru's devotee is accepted along with his kin.
The Guru's devotee contemplates on the Lord with
  fond remembrance.
The Guru's devotee assimilates the essence of the
  Divine Word.
He who knows the mystery of the Word
Only he can explain it to others.
Says Nanak, quitting the evil of ego
He merges into the Lord. (29)

It is for the Guru-conscious that the universe is created,
And the drama of life and death performed.
He who is lost in the Guru's Word
Comes out with flying colours.
Devoted to truth, he arrives home with
    great honour.
Without the True Word one is felicitated not.
Says Nanak, without the Divine Word how can one
    merge into the Divine? (30)

The Guru's devotee attains all the eight
    miraculous powers,
Along with their wisdom.
The Guru's devotee with his acquaintance
    with the truth
Swims across the ocean (of life).
The Guru's devotee knows the ways of truth
    and untruth.
The Guru's devotee knows how to live in the world
And how to give it up.
The Guru's devotee swims across and ferries others.
Says Nanak, remembering the Word, the Guru's
    devotee is emancipated. (31)

Imbued with the Name, one is rid of self-conceit.
Imbued with the Name, one remains devoted to
    the Truth.
Imbued with the Name, one contemplates
    on the means for Union with the Lord.
Imbued with the Name, one arrives at the gate
    of deliverance.

Imbued with the Name, one gains realization of
the three worlds.
Says Nanak, those imbued with the Name live in
peace for ever and ever. (32)

To be imbued with the Name is like entering
into a dialogue with ascetics.
To be imbued with the Name is like doing
perennial penance.
To be imbued with the Name is the true way
of life.
To be imbued with the Name is like gaining
possession of virtuous thoughts.

In the absence of the Name all that we say
is meaningless.
Says Nanak, those devoted to the Name are
always victorious. (33)

It is the supreme Guru who obtains the Name.
Remaining devoted to the Truth is like
practising Yoga.
The Yogis split themselves into twelve sects,
And the recluses into six plus four.
He who kills his conceit with the Divine Word
attains deliverance.
Try to understand this:
Without the Name one is led astray.
Says Nanak, they are great and have
good fortune
Who've enshrined the truth in their heart. (34)

Contemplating upon Him the devotee earns
   the jewel;
And he alone can appreciate its value.
The devotee does what is right.
The devotee is happy remembering the Truthful.
If it so please Him, the devotee sees
   the Unseen. (35)

The devotee remembers God, gives in charity and
   leads a clean life.
The devotee contemplates upon Him constantly.
The devotee is honoured in His Court.
The devotee is fearless,
He remains above the rest.
The devotee does what is virtuous.
Says Nanak, the devotee unites (with God) and
   effects others' unions. (36)

The devotee is acquainted with the Shastras, *the*
   Smritis *and the* Vedas.
The devotee knows what lurks in every mind.
The devotee forgets enmity and opposition.
The devotee is above all reckoning.
The devotee remains intuned with the Lord's Name.
Says Nanak, the devotee truly understands
   the Master. (37)

Without the Guru one comes and goes.
Without the Guru labour bears no fruit.
Without the Guru the mind wavers much.
Without the Guru one is sated not;

It's like consuming poison.
Without the Guru one is bitten by the serpent and
dies half-way.
Says Nanak, without the Guru one suffers
loss after loss. (38)

He whom the Guru blesses is ferried across.
He has his sins washed away and becomes virtuous.
Contemplating on the Guru's Word he is
liberated in the end.
The devotee never comes to be defeated.
The body is the shop and the mind the merchant,
Nanak deals with Truth as ordained by Him. (39)

It was the devotee who built the linking bridge.
Thus Lanka was looted and the demon lashed.
Ram Chand killed the conceited Ravana.
Bhabikhan, the devotee, disclosed the secret.
The devotee ferries even the stones across.
The devotee saved the* "thirty-three crores". (40)

The devotee puts an end to his coming and going.
The devotee earns esteem in heaven.
The devotee distinguishes between good and bad.
The devotee meditates on the Master constantly.
The devotee enters heaven singing His praises.
No one can bar the devotee's passage. (41)

The devotee is blessed with the Name of the
blemishless Lord.

---

* Far too many

The devotee burns his ego with the Divine Word.
The devotee sings praises of the Truthful.
The devotee remains absorbed in the Truth.
The devotee earns fame with the True Name.
The devotee remains cognizant of the world
*   around him.* (42)

"What is its origin?
And what is the faith of the time?
Who is Your Guru?
Whose disciple are you?
What is the Mantra *which keeps you unattached?*
Do tell us, the youth Nanak.
Give us an exposure to the Divine Word
Which can cruise us across the ocean." (43)

Says Nanak:
There was a void in the beginning
The True Lord swayed above.
The Divine Word is the faith of the time;
I meditate on it as a devotee.
I utter the ineffable Name
And it keeps me unattached.
He who is there from time immemorial
*   is my Guru.*
He who meditates on the sacred Word
Such a devotee gets rid of the fire of ego. (44)

"How does one munch iron when one has teeth
*   of wax?*

What should one eat to shed one's ego?
How can one live in a house of snow draped
in fire?
Which is the cave in which the mind
remains steady?
Whom should one deem pervading here and there?
What exercise helps one's mind to concentrate?" (45)

Says Nanak:
Forsaking ego and arrogance helps shed duality.
The world is unkind for the conceited and
the simpleton.
Those who meditate on the Word can munch iron.
He who sees the One Lord inside and out
His fire is abated with the True Guru's
blessings. (46)

He who abides in the fear of the Truthful,
His ego is stilled.
He who meditates on the Divine Word,
Realizes the One God.
Meditating on the Guru's Word
Enshrines truth in one's mind.
The body and the soul are stilled
And get dyed in His hue.
It quenches the fire of lust and anger.
It is His grace that endears one to Him. (47)

"How is the dark, cold mind illumined like
the moon?
How can it shine like the blazing sun?

How can one escape the constant watch of death?
How does the God-conscious save his honour?
Which warrior can control time?
Do tell us, Nanak, your considered view." (48)

Says Nanak:
Meditating on the Name gives the rare shine
of the moon.
The sun and the moon descend into the house to
dispel darkness.
Reliance on the Divine Word
Relieves one from weal and woe.
He Himself cruises you across.
Following the Guru's teachings you imbibe
the truth.
And death dare not devour you. (49)

The Essence of the Name is the supreme virtue;
Without the Name one suffers the agony of death.
Where the essential mind merges with the
soul specific
The mortal is at peace.
After one is rid of duality one enters the House
of God.
When the wind* blows and the sky** rocks
The union is smooth. (50)

God is inside, God is outside,
God pervades the three spheres.

---

* Breath
** The Tenth Gate

He who realises God in the fourth one
is beyond vice and virtue.
He who is aware of the fact of God
permeating every heart;
God, who is the Primordial, Blemishless Lord,
He meditates on His pristine Identity
And gets merged in the Master Creator. (51)

"Everyone talks about the Lord God
But how did the Eternal Master come into being?
How do they look, those who are devoted to
the Lord?"

Says Nanak:
They look like the one they are drawn from.
They are neither born nor do they die.
They neither come nor do they go.
The Guru-conscious can enlighten on it. (52)

Having arrived at the Ninth Door,
One qualifies for the Tenth
Where the eternal melody of the Void is heard
There one confronts the Truthful and merges
into Him.
The True Lord pervades every heart,
He alone reveals the secret of the Divine Word.
One may verify the truth of it. (53)

Meeting the Master bestows peace in its stride.
The Guru-conscious remain awake; they sleep not.
The Limitless Lord dwells in their heart.

Repeating His Name gains salvation;
Emancipation, indeed, lies in His Name.
Those who listen to the Guru turn truthful.
Those who deny themselves meet the Lord.
No more do they linger apart. (54)

"How can one get rid of evil-mindedness?
Why is it that one does not realise the truth
But continues to suffer blows?"

Says Nanak:
He who is
Doomed to die, none may help him.
Without the Divine Word, there is no respect,
    no honour.

"How does one gain awareness and swim across?" (55)

Says Nanak:
The uninitiated, egocentric would understand
    it not,
Evil-mindedness can be warded off by reflecting
    on the Word.
Meeting the True Guru earns salvation. (56)

The conceited who understands not the truth
    comes to grief.
Separated from the Lord,
The misled one suffers the blows of fate.
Submitting to the Divine will is understanding
    the spirit of virtue.
This is how one is lauded in His Court. (57)

"Where does He dwell
He who cruises across the turbulent ocean?
The outbreath is said to travel ten fingers,
How does it happen?
How does one who speaks and sports,
  steady his mind?
How does man see the Unseen?"

Says Nanak:
Listen O Yogi! *Nanak tells nothing but the truth.*
You must discipline your mind.
The devotee must meditate on the Divine Word.
It is His grace which brings about the union.
He understands, He also sees.
Good deeds help one merge into Him. (58)

The Invisible Creator of the world is everywhere.
I see Him wherever I turn.
Like air in the Void, the Virtuous is Omnipresent
And dispels the curse of duality.
The body and the mind are cleansed.
His utterances are nothing but clean.
The Guru's guidance helps one cross the vast ocean.
God has neither any features nor any caste.
He is recognised by His Divine Word. (59)

The True Lord makes the outbreath travel ten
  fingers, O Yogi!
When the devotee speaks, he expounds the truth
And realises the Imperceptible and the Infinite.
When one sheds the three evils and meditates
  on the Word,

The conceit of the mind is dispelled.
He who sees the Lord inside and out
Gets attached to the Divine Word.
When the Unseen Lord comes to be seen,
The breathing channels of the centre,
*   right and left are activated.*
The Lord is above these three avenues,
The True Guru's guidance helps merger
*   in Him.* (60)

"It is said that air sustains life.
What feast does air feed on?
How does one become a sage?
And what makes one an ascetic?"

Says Nanak:
Without the Divine Word the ascetic cannot live,
Nor can his urge for evil be controlled.
Meditating on the word one enjoys the essence
*   of nectar*
And then one remains attached to the Truthful.

"How does one learn to be steady?
What should one eat to remain satiated?"

Says Nanak:
One who treats weal and woe alike,
With the grace of the True Lord
Is not devoured by death. (61)

If one is not dyed in His colour,
If one is not inebriated with His nectar,

Without the Guru's Word,
One is consumed by the inner fire.
If one preserves not one's vitality,
And doesn't cultivate acquaintance with the
      Divine Word,
If one doesn't discipline one's breath,
One cannot meditate on the True Lord.
Uttering the unutterable one maintains
      one's poise;
Only then does one attain the all-pervading. (62)

With the grace of the Guru, one is dyed in
      His colour.
Having tasted nectar, one is absorbed in
      the Truthful.
Having reflected on the Guru the fire inside
      is abated.
Having drunk the rare drink, one attains peace.
Contemplating on the Truthful, the devotee swims
      across the ocean.
Only a few realise this truth. (63)

"Where does the elephant of mind dwell?
And where does the breath of life reside?
Where should the Lord be housed
So that the mind's wavering subsides?"

Says Nanak:
It is His grace that brings about union
And the mind gets steady in its own corner.
When one forsakes conceit, one is cleansed. (64)

As one's mind ceases wandering about,
The Guru-conscious understands the
    Primal Being.
His breath comes to rest in the navel region;
The devotee searches and finds the essence
    of truth.
The Word resides in him constantly,
The Word helps him acquire the light of the
    three spheres.
The longing for the Truthful remedies all ills
And the Truthful quenches all thirst.
The devotee enjoys the unstruck melody
Which very few appreciate.
Nanak tells the truth
Dyed in the colour that never fades. (65)

"When the body and the heart did not exist
Where did the mind dwell?
When the support of the navel-lotus was not there
Where did the breath abide?
When the form and the features did not obtain
How did one meditate on the Divine Word?
When the being of the ovum and sperm was
    not formed
How could one measure the Lord's greatness?
When His colour, garb and features were
    not known
How could one realise the Truthful?"

Says Nanak:
They alone are recluses who meditate on the
    Lord's Name.

The Truest of the True is here and
　　everywhere. (66)

When the heart and body were not there, O Yogi!
The mind abided in the Void.
When the support of the navel-lotus was not there
One resided in one's own self in devotion
　　to the Lord.
When the form, features and caste
　　did not obtain,
One lived in the melody of the Divine.
When there was no earth and no sky,
The Formless Himself pervaded the three spheres.
His colour, clothes and form were contained in
　　the Divine Word.
Without truth no one can endear oneself to
　　the Truthful.
It is difficult, indeed, to talk about all this. (67)

"How did the world come into being?
And what ill will spell its undoing?"

Says Nanak:
The ego compels us to be born.
Forgetting His Name spells suffering.
The devotee reflects upon the Guru's teachings
And kills the ego with the Divine Word.
His body and mind become immaculate
And he, the immaculate, remains devoted to
　　the Truthful.
The recluse remains absorbed in His Name,

With the Divine Word in his heart.
Without the Name one can never be a Yogi.
This must be reflected upon and understood. (68)

Few are those who meditate on the True Name;
Few are those to whom the True Word is revealed.
The Guru-conscious remains absorbed in
*   the Name;*
Few are those who are aware of it.
The Guru-conscious dwells in his own niche.
The Guru-conscious is familiar with the ways
*   of Yogis.*
The Guru-conscious comes to realise the
*   One God.* (69)

Without serving the Guru one cannot be a Yogi.
Without dedicating oneself to the Guru, there is
*   no emancipation.*
Without dedicating oneself to the Guru, the Name
*   cannot be imbibed.*
Without dedicating oneself to the Guru,
*   one suffers anguish and agony.*
Without dedicating oneself to the Guru,
*   one plunges into the darkness of the womb.*
Without dedicating oneself to the Guru,
*   one loses at the hands of death.* (70)

The devotee kills his ego to discipline his mind.
The devotee enshrines the Truthful in his heart.
The devotee annihilates the messenger of death
*   and conquers the world.*

The devotee loses not in the Ultimate Court.
The devotee is the active unifying agent.
The devotee realises the Lord through the
      Divine Word. (71)

O Yogi! *Take note of the essence of the Word.*
Without His Name even Yoga *is not possible.*
Those who meditate on the Name
Remain inebriated day and night.
They find peace and comfort in the Name.
The Name reveals secrets.
The Name fosters spiritual awareness.
Without the Name one may try many a garb,
The True One Himself may mislead him.
O Yogi! *It is the True Guru who blesses us with*
      the Name,
This is Yoga *in itself.*
Dip into your heart and understand
Without the Name there is no emancipation. (72)

You know Your own grandeur and
Your greatness;
None dare evaluate them.
You remain incognito and then reveal Yourself.
You enjoy every change of Yours.
There are ever so many ascetics,
      miracle-workers and their disciples.
They beg Your Name as alms.
They are sacrifice unto a glimpse of Yours.

The Eternal Lord! You stage the play.
Only Your devotees have an inkling of it.
It is You who pervade the entire universe,
There is none other than You! (73)

RAMKALI (SIDH GOSHT) (938-946)

Slok I

The philanthropist doles out ill-gotten wealth
   in charity.
The Guru goes to the people's homes to
   give guidance.
The husband and wife have money as their
   motive of love,
Otherwise they come and go (wherever they fancy).
No one follows the Shastras and the Vedas,
Everyone worships himself.
The Qazi undertakes the administration of justice.
He tells the rosary and utters the name of God,
(And yet) he takes bribes and plays unfair.
If encountered, he has always something to quote
In the language of the Turks which he dins into
   people's ears,
Exploiting and blackmailing them.
The Hindu would plaster his kitchen
And consider himself unsullied and clean.
Who would care for such a Hindu?
The Yogi with matted hair and ash-besmirched
   body
Remains a householder with children clamouring
   around him.
Having trodden on the wrong path, he acquires
   not Yoga.

What has he ridiculed himself for?
Says Nanak, a sign of Kaliyug is
That whoever speaks claims to know everything.

(951)

Slok I

Truthfulness lies neither in distress nor
*   in comfort,*
It lies not in dwelling in water like the nymphs.
It lies not in shaving off the crop of hair,
Nor in wandering about in search of knowledge.
Truthfulness lies neither in living in jungles
*   nor in caves;*
Torturing the body is deceiving oneself.
It lies not in elephants kept chained at
*   your house,*
Nor in droves of grazing cows.
He acquires it whom the one who is
*   proficient imparts.*
The one who is given is said to have arrived.
Says Nanak, he alone is commended
Who has the Divine Word enshrined in him.

"All the hearts are mine," says the Lord,
I dwell in them."
Who can retrieve him whom I mislead?
None dare mislead him whom I show the way,
He whom I misdirect at the outset,
Can never be brought back on to the right path."

(952)

Slok I

Hearken O man! Nanak tells you the truth.
With His logbook open before Him
God must examine your account.
The non-believers with their dues
Must come to grief;
Azrael, the messenger of death,
Takes charge of them.
Entangled in narrow lanes
They would not know how to extricate themselves.
Says Nanak, the false must perish
And the true ones should survive.

(953)

Slok I

Cleaned, ginned, carded, spun and woven,
Scissored in pieces, and washed snow-white.
The iron shears, the tailor pares,
The needle and thread stitch it.
The like of it, the disgraced is redeemed,
By singing His praises he is rejuvenated.
When worn-out cloth is torn
It is stitched again with needle and thread.
It may, however, last not for a month or even
    a fortnight;
At times not even for an hour or a moment.
The truth never grows old.
Once stitched it wears out not.
Says Nanak, my Master is the truest of the true,
He can be testified as such.

(955)

Raga Maru

Maru

Some call me a goblin and others a demon.
Yet some others see in Nanak a simpleton.
Nanak, the crazy, has gone insane for his Master.
I know none other than God.
He is insane who becomes obsessed in his fear.
Except the Lord he accepts none else.
He is insane who serves the One God only.
He abides by his Master, cares not for anyone else.
He is insane who loves his Lord,
Thinks poorly of himself and lauds the rest of
*   the world.*

(991)

Maru I

The Ganga, the Yamuna, Brindaban and Kedarnath,
Varanasi, Mathura, Puri and Dwarka,
Where the Ganga meets the ocean and the
*   confluence of Triveni,*
Together with the sixty-eight places of pilgrimage,
All are contained in the Lord.
He is an ascetic, a seeker and a sage,
The sovereign with His select advisers.
The Judge-God sits on the throne,
Dispelling doubts and misconceptions.

He is the Qazi *and the* Mulla.
Infallible, He never makes a mistake.
Kind and compassionate Provider
He harbours no enmity.
He whom He takes kindly to, glorifies Him.
The Giver to all with not an iota of
discrimination.
The Immaculate Lord pervades everything,
and is Omnipresent,
In both manifest and unmanifest forms.
How can I measure the Inaccessible and the Infinite?
He is the True Creator and Destroyer of the ego.
Whom He takes kindly to He unites;
He gets together those who are Guru-conscious.
Brahma, Vishnu and Shiva wait on Him.
They serve the Immeasurable and
the Incomprehensible.
There are ever so many who clamour and crowd
at His gate.
I have no count of them.
Great is His reputation and as great His Word;
None other is matched or excelled in the Vedas and
the Puranas.
Truth is my capital and I sing His praises.
I have nothing else to rely upon.
The True One was there from time immemorial.
He is there today and He will be there ever after;
He never died nor will He ever die.
Nanak, the meek, entreats:
Look within, you will find Him there enshrined.

(1022)

Maru I

The True One unites;
The Divine Word is the Media.
When it pleases Him, He does it on His own.
His light pervades the three worlds.
There is none other than He.
I serve the One whose slave I am.
I propitiate the Invisible and the Inscrutable,
Through the Divine Word.
A great benefactor of His devotees,
He forgives; this being His wont.
There is no end to the favours granted by the
*   Truthful.*
The faithless receive and they deny it.
They understand not the source,
Cultivate not the truth,
And are misled by doubts and deception.
The Guru-conscious remains absorbed in
*   Him day and night.*
The Guru-conscious is devoted to the Truthful.
The conceited lies asleep and is looted.
The Guru-conscious remains unharmed.
The false one comes and goes.
Given to falsehood, he indulges in misdeeds.
Those blessed with the Divine Word are lauded in
*   His Court.*
The Guru-conscious remains absorbed in shabd.
The false are exploited and cheated by swindlers.
The way the stray cattle ravage a crop.
Without the Name nothing is agreeable to
*   the palate.*

Forgetting the Lord leads to suffering.
The diet of truth is most wholesome.
The possession of the jewel of the Name is the
    true honour.
He who understands himself realises God.
His light blends with the Light Divine.
He who forgets the Name comes to grief.
Trying to be clever doesn't dispel doubts.
Overloaded with the burden of sin,
Without remembering Him,
One dies a painful, lingering death.
There is none free from contention
    and controversy.
I'll salute him if you were to show me one.
The Lord God is won by dedicating oneself to
    Him body and soul.
Then one lives in harmony with Him.
No one can measure the greatness of God.
He who calls himself great is undone by
    his conceit.
There is no limit to the bounties of the Truthful;
The entire world is created by Him.
(Worldly) greatness has no charm for the
    Great Lord;
He creates and provides.
The kind-hearted Benefactor never distances Himself;
If He so desires, one can meet Him unawares.
There are some who are grief-stricken,
Others are afflicted with ailments;
It is all as pleases Him.
With loving devotion and abiding by His advice

One hears the unstruck melody.
Some roam about naked and hungry.
Some die in obstinacy without any purpose;
They know not the truth of the good and the evil
It is the Divine Word which brings about
    the realization of truth.
Some bathe at places of pilgrimage and eat not,
Others sit by the fire they make and
    torture themselves.
Without the Name of the Lord there is
    no emancipation,
There is no cruising across.
He who quits the path of the Guru goes astray,
The conceited one remembers not the Lord and
    wastes away
In evil deeds and false practices.
Falsehood and death are sworn enemies.
Man comes and goes as commanded by God.
He who accepts His command blends with Truth.
Prays Nanak, may I imbibe the Truth which I cherish
And my deeds be as divinely directed?

                                        (1024-25)

Maru I

I come to Your protection, my Lord!
You are all-powerful, kind, and the killer of evil.
Nobody knows Your ways.
You are the embodiment of perfection,
A consummate Creator.
Right from the beginning and even before

You have sustained the universe.
O my compassionate Lord of unmatched charm!
It is You who dwell in every heart.
It works the way You desire;
Whatever happens is due Your pleasure.
Your light illumines my inside.
O Sustainer of the world!
Everyone cherishes Your nectar.
You are the giver and You are the taker,
You are the gracious Master of the three worlds.
Having created the world, the Lord staged
      a drama;
He materialised man from air, water and fire,
And the nine doors in the city of the body,
With the tenth kept barred.
He also created the four frightful rivers of fire,
Which only a rare cherisher of the Word
      understands.
The misled materialist is drowned or burnt,
Those protected by the Guru remain devoted to Him
Water, fire, air, earth and sky,
These five elements constitute the human being.
He who is imbued with the Divine Word,
Sheds Maya, ego and duality.
Absorbed in the Guru's Word, the mind is
      entranced.
What other support is there besides His Name?
The temple of the body is being ravaged by thieves,
But the reprobate is not aware of the demon.
There are malignant spirits and goblins
Who pick up devilish quarrels.

Without the understanding of the Divine Word
One comes and goes.
Both coming and going are without any dignity.
The body of the liar is like a heap of
    saltpetre ash.
What honour can there be without the Name?
He remains a captive in all the four ages
Under the watchful eye of the Messenger of Death.
Caught by the demon, he is punished;
The sinner finds no salvation.
He cries his heart out and wails,
Like a fish entangled in the hook.
The non-believer mounts the gallows unlamented,
Blinded (with conceit) the miserable wretch gets
    into the clutches of Yama.
Without the Divine Name there is no deliverance,
One goes on wasting, day by day.
In the absence of the True Guru, none
    befriends you.
It is the Lord who protects you here and hereafter.
When He blesses you with His Name,
It is like water mixing with water.
Devotees gone astray are advised by the Guru;
He puts those misled on the right path.
One should serve the Guru day and night,
He who is the reliever of pain and a
    constant companion.
How can a poor mortal propitiate God?
Even Brahma, Indra and Shiva know
    not the way.
How can one comprehend the Incomprehensible?

He realises Him whom He Himself blesses.
He who loves the Lord from the core of his heart,
He is granted His glimpse.
He who is devoted to the Divine Word,
He is blessed with Union.
He who keeps the bright light burning,
    day and night
Enshrined in his heart,
He alone understands Him.
His understanding is a feast of the sweetest elixir;
He who tastes it has a vision of the Lord.
A glimpse of the Lord brings about the Union;
All the anxieties melt as one merges in God.
They are blessed who serve the True Guru.
They recognise God in every heart.
Nanak pleads for the Guru's adoration
In order to find the company of Godmen,
Those who have known the True Guru.

(1031-32)

Maru I

For countless ages there prevailed utter darkness;
No earth, no sky, only God's will.
No day, no night, neither the moon nor the sun,
He sat in a trance in the Vast Void.
There was no eating, no speaking.
 There was no water, no air,
No creation, no destruction,
No coming, no going,
There were no planets, no underworld,

None of the seven seas
With rivers flowing into them.
There were no planes: higher, middle or lower,
Not hell nor heaven, not any hour of death.
No suffering, no bliss,
No birth, no death.
No entry, no exit.
There was no Brahma, no Vishnu, no Shiva.
Excepting Him none else was in view.
Neither was there any female, nor any male
Born with any caste.
Nor anyone underwent pain or pleasure.
There was no celibate, no saint,
Nor anyone living in the forest dwelling.
Neither any ascetic, nor any seeker,
Nor those who look for pleasure.
Neither was there any Yogi *nor any*
    itinerant recluse.
There was none in any other garb,
Nor anyone claiming to be the master Yogi,
There was no meditation, no penance,
No discipline, no fasting, no worship.
No one called or considered himself alien.
He was delighted at having created Himself.
He assessed His own performance Himself.
There was no purification, no restraint,
Neither any rosary nor any sweet basil.
There were no milkmaids, no Krishna,
No cows, no cowherdsmen.
There were no spells, no mantras,
No hypocrisy, none beat his own drum.

There was no Karma, no Dharma,
No Maya, no gadfly of Mammon.
The caste and (pride of) birth were nowhere.
There was no entanglement of attachment, no fear
*   of death.*
Nobody meditated on anyone else.
There was no slandering, no praise.
There was no soul nor was there life.
There was no Gorakh nor anyone with the
*   name Machhandar.*
There was no Divine lore nor spiritual practice.
Neither (pride of) superior birth
Nor the need to render account.
There were no classes, no distinguishing garbs.
No Brahmins, no Kshatriyas.
No deity, no shrine, no cow nor any
*   primary spell.*
There were no havan ceremonies,
No bathing at the places of pilgrimage.
Nor did anyone perform any worship.
There was no mulla, no qazi,
Neither sheikh nor penitent,
No one made pilgrimage to Mecca.
There were no subjects, no ruler,
None with worldly pride,
No one styling himself big.
There was no love, no devotion.
Neither Shiva nor Shakti.
There were no friends,
Nor anyone related by blood or other ties.
He was the moneylender and the trader;
This is how he delighted Himself.

There were no Vedas, no Islamic scriptures,
No Shastras, no Smritis,
There was no reading of the Puranas.
At dawn or sunset.
The Incomprehensible Lord was Himself the
* preacher,*
And Himself the speaker.
The Unseen saw everything.
When He so desired, He created the universe,
And sustained the firmament without support.
Created Brahma, Vishnu and Shiva
And also the fascination for Maya.
Few are there whom the Guru has revealed this.
Having created the universe,
The Lord swayed above it.
He brought about planets, the hemisphere
* and the underworld*
And from the Unknowable came to be known.
No one knows His extent.

The Great Guru Himself inculcates
* understanding.*
Says Nanak, those in trance are imbued
* with the Truth.*
Singing His Praises, they become ecstatic.

(1035-36)

Slok I

*Merit offered without due appreciation is sold
   cheap.
When it finds a proper customer, a fortune
   it fetches.*

*Virtue attracts the virtuous and merges with the
   True Guru.
Invaluable it is, bargained, can't be in
   the bazaar.*

(1086-87)

Raga Tukhari
Barah Mah
(The Twelve Months of the Year)

There is but one God.
Who is realised through the grace of the True God.

Listen my beloved Lord.
One reaps the rewards of one's past deeds.
Sorrow and happiness come as You dispense them.
This Creation is Yours.
I am nobody.
I may live not for a moment without You.
Without You, my love, I am miserable.
Friendless, I sip Nectar with the Guru-conscious.
The Formless! You are contained in
*   Your Creation.*
Those who meditate on You,
Do whatever is good.
Nanak, the bride has set her eyes on Your path,
The Master! You must take notice of it. (1)

(1107)

The sparrow hawk calls her love,
So does the cuckoo.
The bride enjoys every pleasure

185

Clung to her love.
Blessed as she is.
She, indeed, is a happy bride.
Creating the nine houses,
With Your mansion (the tenth) above them,
You reside in it,
Enemy of Evil!
Everything here is Yours, my beloved!
I am intoxicated in Your company, day and night.
The sparrow hawk calls to her love;
So does the cuckoo. (2)

(1107)

Listen, my beloved Lord!
I am lost in Your love.
I am absorbed in You every moment in body
      and mind.
I forget You not for a stance.
How can I forget You?
You, unto whom I am a sacrifice?
I live by singing Your praises.
None belongs to me,
Nor do I belong to anyone.
I can live not without You, my Master.
I come to You for refuge.
Your feet are my seat.
My body is thereby sanctified.
Nanak has found lasting peace,
The Guru's Word is my heart's anchor. (3)

(1107)

It rains Nectar
In delightful drops.
By a happenstance, I met the Master
And I fell in love with Him at first sight.
He comes home when he pleases;
Overjoyed, the bride sings His praises;
The brides enjoy their grooms under every roof,
How is it that my Master has forgotten me?
The clouds have gathered low,
They pour as they please,
It gladdens my mind and soul.
Says Nanak, when the ambrosial Word rains,
The Master comes home gracefully (4)

(1107)

(The month of) Chet is welcome,
It comes with spring and the pretty bumble-bee,
The plants in the orchard are in blossom,
My Lord should now come home!
Without the spouse, how can the bride feel happy?
She wastes away suffering the pangs of
*   separation.*
With the kokil singing her melody in the mango tree,
The ache in my body becomes unbearable.
The bumble-bee flitting the flowering bough;
I can bear it not,
I am dying, my mother!
Says Nanak, Chet can bring joys galore
If the bride finds her spouse back home. (5)

(1108)

Baisakh is pleasant
With boughs laden with fresh leaves.
The bride wistfully looks at the door
Waiting for her God-lover to come home,
And cruise her across the turbulent ocean.
Without Him, she is worth not a shell.
If You were to cherish me
Who would dare measure my merit?
I glance at You longingly
And make a show of it.
You are not far.
You live within me.
I've come to recognise my Master's mansion.
Says Nanak, whoever meets the Lord in the month
      of Baisakh,
It is on account of his meditation on the
Divine Word. (6)

                                                    (1108)

Propitious is the month of Jeth.
How can one forget one's love?
In supplication, her being burns like a furnace.
As she implores, she sings his praises.
Singing praises she endears herself to him.
However, the revered Recluse resides in
      His palace.
She can go to Him only if He permits.
How can the helpless, the meek, arrive at the
Palace of Pleasure

Without the Lord's intervention?
Says Nanak, She who resembles Him in looks
The fortunate one meets the Lord in the month of
    Jeth. (7)

(1108)

Frightful is (the month of) Asad
When the Sun blazes in the sky.
The earth is in agony
Parched with burning fire;
They worry themselves to death
And yet the Sun doesn't relent.
Its chariot moves on as the bride looks for shade.
The grasshoppers wail in the forest.
She who goes with her load of sins comes to grief.
The one who is truthful enjoys peace.
Nanak would live and die with Him
To whom he has dedicated himself. (8)

(1108)

Sawan is the month of rejoicing.
It is the time when dark clouds pour.
I long for my Love but my Lord is away;
My spouse being away, I suffer his pangs.
The lightning flashes and frightens.
All alone in my bed I grieve,
The pain is killing, my mother!
Without God, leave aside sleep or hunger
I wear not clothes on my body.
Says Nanak, she is the happy bride,
Who is identified with the person of her spouse. (9)

(1108)

In (the month of) Bhadon her robust youth leads
*   her astray;*
And she regrets it.
There is water in pools and plains.
The rainy season is for rejoicing.
It rains during the dark night;
How can the young bride be at peace?
The frogs and peacocks cry aloud.
The pied cuckoo calls to her sweetheart.
Snakes sting at every step.
Mosquitoes bite and the pools are brimful.
How can one feel happy without love?
Says Nanak, ask your Guru and do likewise,
Go the way He directs. (10)

(1108)

Come my Lord, it's the month of Assu!
Your love pines for You.
But one can meet You only if You so please,
It's no use asking anyone else.
Taking to falsehood is alienating the spouse.
How can a dry reed blossom?
Having weathered summer, I've winter in store;
My mind is in a peculiar predicament.
The boughs all around the ten sides are in bloom,
That which ripens steadily is sweet.
Says Nanak, do meet me in Assu, my love!
I have my Guru as my mediator. (11)

(1109)

In Katak you get what is destined for you.
The lamp lit with truth burns steadily.
Love is the oil in the lamp,
It unites the bride with the groom.
The bride is then blessed and rejoices.
Dying in misdeeds she dies not.
Death in virtue earns true liberation.
Meditating on the Divine Word
She sits still at home
With hope resting on the Lord-God.
Prays Nanak, my Master, come and meet me,
Untying the locks of evil.
A moment now appears like six months. (12)

(1109)

The month of Maghar is welcome for those
Who, singing His praises, are absorbed in Him.
The virtuous sing His praises
She endears herself to the Lord for ever and ever.
My Creator is steady, sensitive and sagacious,
The world around us is unstable.
Those who are in the know meditate on Him;
They get absorbed in Him
And become His favourites.
I've heard songs and music and poets
    reciting poems
But it's listening to the Lord's Name that makes
    sorrows disappear.
Says Nanak, only that bride is loved by her groom
Who meditates on His Name from the core of
    her heart. (13)

(1109)

In the month of Poh it snows.
The trees and grass are sucked dry.
Why don't You come, my Lord?
You dwell in my heart, my body and on my tongue.
God, the Creator of the world, resides in me.
I enjoy Him meditating on His Name.
His light kindles in all those
Whether egg-born, foetus-born, sweat-born or self-
born.
Do give me a glimpse, my compassionate Lord,
So that I qualify for salvation.
Says Nanak, he who loves enjoys love,
He who is devoted endears himself to Him. (14)

(1109)

Realising that inside me I have a shrine
I am sanctified in the month of Magh.
Imbibing His qualities, I've met my Love.
I've identified myself with His person.
Listen, my Love!
Now that I have acquired Your virtues,
If You please,
May I have a dip in Your pool?
You are the confluence of the Ganga and the
Yamuna,
You also embrace the seven seas.
Charity, alms-giving and the worship of God
Remain the same from age to age.
Says Nanak, meditating on God in Magh,
Is the quintessence of bathing at sixty eight
shrines. (15)

(1109)

Those who are blessed with love in Phagun
Are at peace with themselves.
Rid of the ego, they are happy day and night.
I've quit my conceit as ordained,
Do be kind and come back home.
In Your absence, I dressed and dressed
And yet could not enter Your palace.
When it pleased You, however,
I adorned myself with necklaces, strings of pearls,
*   perfume and silk.*
Thus did Nanak meet his Master,
The bride found her groom at home. (16)

(1109)

If the Truthful were to visit me in His sublime grace
All the twelve months, the seasons and the
*   lunar days would be blessed.*
If the Lord were to come, all the problems
*   would be solved.*
The Creator knows best how to do it.
I am His devotee and He has groomed me;
Having met Him, I relish His company.
Blessed is the bed where my Lord courts me,
It is good fortune for the Guru-conscious.
Says Nanak, she enjoys her love day and night;
With God as her groom, she remains an
*   eternal bride.* (17)

(1109-10)

Tukhari I

You, with the bewitching eyes,
Take care, the accursed one!
In the first watch the night is dark,
Your turn, too, can come.
When your turn comes,
Who will wake you?
Asleep, Death would suck your blood.
In the dark night
Who would care for you?
The thief will break into your house.
O my Saviour, Inaccessible and Infinite!
Pray, listen to my supplicaiton.
Nanak, the stupid, remembers you not,
How will he find his way in the dark night? (1)

It is the second watch.
You may be fast asleep when you should wake up.
Take care, the accursed one!
Your crop is being ravaged.
Look after your crop and keep faith in God.
If you are awake the thief dares not enter.
The messenger of death will not waylay you,
Nor will you come to grief.

The dread of death would disappear.
The lamps of the Sun and the Moon
Are lit at the Guru's door.
With a truthful mind meditate on Him.
Nanak, the stupid, will still not heed,
How would he find peace
Given to somone else as he is? (2)

In the third watch, you are still asleep,
Lost in money, progeny and spouse,
Endeared to the world.
Pecking your feed, you are caught in a net,
It is meditating on the Name
That will bring you peace.
The devotee is not devoured by death.
There is no escape from the tortures of
     birth and death.
Without the Name it is unmitigated agony.
Says Nanak, in the third watch
All the three species of mortals
Are engrossed in temptation. (3)

It is the fourth watch.
The day of death may dawn any moment.
They who are awake day and night
Their houses remain safe.
Those who, under the Guru's advice,
Meditate on His Name,
Their nights are peaceful.
Those who repeat the the Guru's Word
Are not born again.

They attain God, the Protector.
The hands shake,
The feet and the rest of the frame flounder,
The sight is dimmed
And the body is reduced to dust.
Says Nanak, without God's Name in his mind
Man is unhappy in all the four stages. (4)

The knot is loosened,
Get up,
The summons have arrived.
Enough of enjoyment and comfort.
You are to be shackled and led away.
You are to be manacled as ordained by God
Whom you can neither see nor hear.
Everyone must proceed in his turn.
When the crop is ripe, it is mowed.
You will be asked to account for your every hour,
    every moment.
And rewarded for good or bad deeds.
Says Nanak, God arranges in such a way
That saints are united with the Lord
By the ties of the Divine Word. (5)

(1110)

Raga Bhairo

Bhairo I Sector I

Nothing happens unless You permit it.
You do what You desire.
What should I say?
I can't say much.
It's all as per Your design.
If I have to ask for anything
It is You I approach.
To whom shall I address a prayer?
I talk about You,
Listen to Your Word.
You are the greatest of all.
You alone know Yourself.
You do everything Yourself,
And make others do as You desire.
Thus does Nanak see his Creator and Destroyer.

(1125)

Basant I Sector I

Among the months most auspicious is Basant
That marks the advent of Spring;
Meditating on the Master
I am ever in bloom.
Listen, innocent one!
Shake off your conceit.
Kill your ego and meditate on Him.
Match your virtues with those of the Lord.
Your deeds are the tree, God's Name the branch,
Your faith the flower, and revelation the fruit.
Meeting the Lord are the leaves
And getting rid of pride its thick shade.
He who realises the Lord's splendour
Hears the Divine Word,
Utters His True Name,
He is bequeathed the Lord's bounties.
His mind comes to be concentrated on Him.
The months and seasons come and go,
You must do good deeds.
Says Nanak, those who are devoted to Him,
They remain ever green, they never die.

(1168)

Basant I

Your kitchen square may be all gold
Your vessels golden.
The silver lines of the square
May extend far.

You may have water from the Ganga
And the fire of the Carrissa Carandas.
You may feed yourself with
Rice cooked in milk.
All this amounts to nothing,
If you have not imbibed the True Name.
Even if eighteen Puranas
Have been copied out by you,
Even if you know the four Vedas by heart,
Even if you bathe at holy places
On festive days
And give in charity to the needy,
You observe fasts and are disciplined day
    and night,
You may be a Qazi or a Mulla,
A Yogi, a wandering seer,
Or one clad in ochre-coloured garments,
You may be a family man, following the
    religious rites;
But without realising the Lord
You are caught and driven away.
The mortals have their fate predetermined,
Decisions taken are based on one's deeds.
It is the ignorant and the foolish who listen not
    to Him.
Says Nanak, the True One has no end of those
    who heed Him.

(1169)

Basant I

Don't you get misled
By the pride of having smeared your body
    with ash.
Yoga *doesn't consist in roaming about naked.*
Oh foolish One! Why have you forgotten the
    Lord's Name?
It's the only thing that will come to your
    rescue in the end;
Ask your Guru and reflect on it.
Wherever you look, you will find the Master of
    the universe.
What do I say, when there is none else?
The high caste and the honour
Are the blessings of His Name.
Why should you feel elated with riches
    and property?
At the time of your departure nothing will
    accompany you.
Annihilate the five evils
And concentrate on Him;
This is the secret of the yogic way of living.
Your mind is swollen with pride;
Oh stupid one! You remember not God
Who can ordain your emancipation.
Don't you forget God,
Lest you fall into the clutches of death.
Misled! You will suffer in the end;
Meditating on the Divine Word will kill your ego
And true Yoga will be your guide.

You remember not Him who has blessed you
*   with life.*
Oh stupid one! Yoga *is not to be found at the*
*   graveyard or cremation ground.*
Guru Nanak tells the truth,
Open your eyes and embrace it.

(1189-90)

Basant Hindol I Sector 2

Having established nine planets, seven seas,
*   fourteen continents,*
Three spheres and four ages,
God seated the four species of Creation in
*   His mansion,*
Giving four lamps in their hands,
One lamp in each hand.
O my Merciful, Madhusudan, Madho,
Such is Your might!
The light in every home is your physical force
While your righteousness rules over it.
The earth is an all-time cooking cauldron
And destiny Your store-keeper.
The discontented asks for more and more,
The eclectic thus humiliates himself.
Avarice is the dark dungeon,
Evil deeds, fetters on the feet.
The love of riches is like the blows of a mallet;
The sins acting as watchmen
Good or bad, man is what You make him.
The Primal Lord is called Allah these days;

It is the age of Sheikhs.
The Hindu temples and their gods are taxed,
Such is the way of the world.
The ablution pot, the call to prayer and the
     prayer-mat,
God has taken to garments blue.
"Mian" is how they address each other
     in every home,
Their language is altogether different.
If You have become a Muslim,
What about us?
You will be salaamed from all the four quarters
Your praises will be sung in every home.
Going on pilgrimages, reading the Smritis
     and giving alms
May earn us something like a day's wages.
Nanak was bestowed honour,
Remembering Him just for a moment.

(1190-91)

Raga Sarang

Slok I

*He is pleased neither with music, vocal or
     instrumental,
Nor with reciting the* Vedas.
*He is pleased neither with wisdom and knowledge,
Nor with living a luxurious life.
He is pleased neither with pilgrimages
Nor with remaining unclothed.
He is pleased neither with philanthropy,
Nor with giving alms at random.
He is pleased not with sitting all alone in
     wilderness.
He is pleased not with fighting evil
Until the hero's end.
He is pleased not with people becoming the
dust of His feet.
It is the measure of your love that is
     recorded there.
Says Nanak, He is pleased with the True
Name alone.*

(1237)

Slok I

There is no impurity in* music
Nor in the Vedas.
There is no impurity in the Moon, the Sun
And their various phases.
There is no impurity in corn
Nor in ablution (not done properly).
There is no impurity in rain
Which falls all over.
There is no impurity in earth
Nor in water.
There is no impurity in the air
Contained in everything.
Says Nanak, one without the Guru is impure.
Turning away from the Lord
The mouth is defiled.

(1240)

Says Nanak, a mouthful of water cleanses
If one knows how to do it.
For the wise, the mouthful of water is knowledge,
For the Yogi *it is sanctity.*
A mouthful of water is contentment for
*   the Brahmin,*
And for the householder truth and charity.
The mouthful of water is justice for the ruler,
And for the learned, reflection on the Truthful.
The water doesn't cleanse the mind,

---

*   As believed in Islam

Drinking it with the mouth only quenches thirst.
Water is the source of all creation
And it is in water that everything dissolves.

(1240)

Slok I

Kaliyug has the face of a dog,
Carrion is its feed.
It barks out lies and untruths
With no respect for Dharma.
Those who are respected not in life,
They carry no fair name after death.
Says Nanak, what is destined must happen;
What happens is ordained by the Creator.

The women have taken to intellectual pursuits,
And men to violence.
Culture, discipline and piety are forgotten,
People eat what they can't assimilate.
Modesty has been given a go by
Along with the sense of self-respect.
Says Nanak, God alone is true,
Don't look for another Truthful One.

(1242-43)

Slok I

Death is no respector of time,
Hour or the day.
Some have loaded, some have left after loading,

Some others are still loading.
(Of these) some have been treated sternly,
Some others received civil treatment.
They leave their splendid mansions
Along with their armies and trumpets.
Says Nanak, the heap of dust
Comes to be reduced to dust again.

It was a citadel of clay,
Says Nanak, it collapsed like so much mud.
There was a thief lurking inside,
Like falsehood covering falsehood.

(1244)

Slok I

Singing hymns without insight
(Is like) a starving **Mulla** *turning his house*
  into a mosque,
An unemployed getting his ears pierced
To become a mendicant and lose his caste.
He who calls himself Guru or Pir
And goes about begging,
Don't you ever fall at his feet.
He who labours, earns and gives in charity,
Says Nanak, he has understood the Truthful One.

(1245)

Raga Malar

Malar I

The bride who has not known the love of
    her groom
Bewails, her body wasting away.
She gets frustrated, caught in the noose of
    her Karma.
Without the Guru, she is drowned in doubts.

My love is visiting me,
The clouds must open up and pour.
I am sacrifice unto my beloved Guru
Who has brought about this union,.
My love for the Lord is ever new,
My devotion to Him is a delight, day and night.
A glimpse of the Guru and I am emancipated,
I am glorified for ever and ever.
O Lord of the three worlds!
I am Yours;
I am Yours and You are mine.
Meeting the True Guru, one attains
    the Immaculate.
There is no visiting the world again.

The bride who is delighted to see her groom,
Her doing herself up is justified.
Truly devoted to the Casteless and
    Immaculate Lord,
She has the Divine Name as her support.
She attains emancipation;
Her groom undoes her shackles.
Meditating on the Name, she attains respectability.
Says Nanak, with the Lord's Name in her heart,
The Guru-conscious merges in the Master.

(1255)

Malar I

Separation is painful;
Painful also is hunger.
The dreadful blow of death is likewise painful;
Painful is the malady that wastes away the body.
The poor physician knows no cure for it.

The poor physician knows no cure for it.
With the pain persisting, the body aches.
There is no remedy for this affliction.

Forgetting the Master, I indulged in
    merry-making
Which caused many an ailment.
The misled mortal is penalised.
The poor physician has no cure for it.

The sandalwood tree exudes fragrance
The way man breathes.

How long does it take for the breath to stop
After which there is no merry-making?

If it has an iota of the Name of the Immaculate,
The body shines like gold.
It is as spotless as a swan.

All the ills and aches are shed.
Says Nanak, the Divine Name is a great healer.

(1256)

Malar I

You wear white garments.
You are polite in speech.
You have a sharp nose.
Your eyes are dark.
Sister! Have you ever met the Lord?

I take a flight and soar in the sky.
I do it with the blessings of my mighty Lord.
I behold the sea and the land,
Mountains and riverbanks.
In every nook and corner I find my Master.

He who has created this body and the wings,
Has also infused the longing for flying.
If He is merciful, I take courage.
I see what He wishes me to see.

The body and the wings will die not.
They are compounds of air, water and fire.

Says Nanak, if you are fortunate
You remember Him under the Guru's guidance
And this body merges in Truth.

(1257)

Slok I

Says Nanak, if it rains in the month of Sawan,
Four species are overjoyed:
The snake, the deer, the fish
And those fond of merry-making.

Says Nanak, if it rains in the month of Sawan,
Four species suffer separation:
The calf, the poor,
The wayfarer and servants.

(1279)

Slok I

The physician has been sent for
To prescribe a remedy;
He pulls my arm
And feels the pulse.
A simpleton, the physician knows not
The ache is deep in the heart!

(1279)

Slok I

Fools confer robes of honour
And the shameless accept them.

A mouse with a winnowing-basket tied to
    his waist
Cannot be contained in a hole.
Those who bless others must die;
Also those who are blessed.
Nanak knows not the ways of God,
Where they come from and where they go.
I understand the rabi crop for remembering
    His Name,
Also the kharif crop for meditating on the
    True Name.
I go to the Master's Court
And have my pardon-deed signed.
Many are the doors of the world,
Through which many come and go.
Many are those who ask for favours;
And many who gain them and die.

                                    (1286)

Pauri

Some repair to the forest
And utter not a word.
Some others sit in ice-cold water
Fracturing the frozen surface.
There are those who smear ash on their body
And would not wash it clean.
There are yet others who, with their long
    matted hair,
Wear a weird look,
And thus disgrace their clan.

There are some who roam about naked day
    and night,
They sleep not.
There are those who singe their limbs with fire,
Torturing themselves.
Without His Name the body is mere dust;
You may do anything with it.
Those who serve the True Guru,
Are honoured at the Master's Court.

(1284-85)

Pauri

He is the True Invisible, Inscrutable Lord.
He is not pleased with obstinacy.
Some indulge in musical performances;
He remains unmoved.
There are others who dance to a tune;
It is no worship of God.
Those who eat not are foolish.
What can be done for them?
Man's thirst is limitless,
In no way can it be quenched.
There are those who are bound by rituals,
They die worrying about them.
The gain of this world is His Name
And the sip of Amrit.
The Guru-conscious acquire all this
Through love and devotion.

(1285)

Slok I

The elephant eats a hundred maunds of clarified
    butter and molasses.
And another five hundred maunds of corn.
He belches, blows and raises dust,
Albeit he regrets the moment his breathing stops.
The blind die in self-conceit;
Those who are devoted to the Master
    are favoured.
Pecking half a corn, the sparrow chirps, flying high
    in the sky.
God is pleased with the one who remembers
    His Name.
The mighty tiger kills hundreds of deers which
    others eat.
Overbearing, he wouldn't enter his den.
Albeit regrets the moment his breathing stops.
Whom does the blind beast impress with his roar?
The Master approves it not.
The milk-weed cricket adores the milk-weed
And eats its leaves perching on it.
God is pleased with one who remembers His Name.
Says Nanak, in the four days of the world
The pursuit of pleasure spells pain.
There are many who talk about it,
But none can renounce the world.
The fly gives its life for its weakness for sweets.
Those whom You protect, no harm comes to them.
They cross the dreadful ocean in Your fear.

                        (1286)

Slok I

There is alliance between beauty and lust
The way the hungry man has with dainty dishes.
The greedy coming across wealth
Get engrossed in it,
The way one who is sleepy
Doesn't mind a narrow bed.
He who is angry howls and is humiliated.
Blinded by wrath, he shouts in vain.
Says Nanak, it is best to remain quiet;
Without the Name all that the mouth
    utters is mere froth.

Power, property, beauty, high caste and youth,
They are the five thugs.
The thugs have swindled the world.
They have spared no one's honour.
Those who come to the Guru's care,
Vanquish all these thugs.
Says Nanak, those who are not fortunate enough,
Are cheated many a time.

(1288)

Slok I

Implanted by flesh, conceived in flesh,
You nested in flesh.
When infused with life
Your mouth, bones, skin and body were created
    in flesh.

Emerging out of the flesh (of the womb)
You sucked breasts of flesh.
Your mouth is of flesh; of flesh is your tongue.
It is with flesh that you breathe.
As you grow, you wed
And bring home flesh.
The flesh gives birth to flesh.
All your relatives have ties of flesh.
It is when one meets the True Guru
That things get sorted out;
There is no emancipation on one's own.
Says Nanak, mere talking leads to nothing.

Fools fight for flesh
With neither gnosis nor meditation.
They know not what is flesh and
     what is not
And what it is to be sinful.
They slaughtered a rhinoceros for their sacred feast,
This was the way of the gods.
Those who give up eating meat
And hold their nose to shut out its smell,
Swallow human beings in the dark.
The hypocrites make a show of it;
They have nothing to do with gnosis
     or meditation.
Says Nanak, it's no use talking to the blind,
If you do, it goes unheeded.
He is blind who acts blind;
He has no mental eyes.
Born out of the blood of the mother and father

And yet they eat not fish nor meat.
When the husband and wife meet at night,
They indulge in the not so elevating game of flesh.

Born of flesh and conceived in flesh,
We are vessels of flesh,
Without gnosis or meditation.
O Pandit! You call yourself learned.
The flesh belonging to others is bad
That which is your own is good?
All creation owes its existence to flesh;
The soul makes its abode in it.
Those whose Guru is blind
They eat not what they should eat.
And they eat what they should not.
Born out of flesh and conceived in flesh,
We are the vessels of flesh.
Wanting in gnosis and meditation
O Pandit! You call yourself learned.
Eating meat is permissible in the Puranas.
Meat-eating is allowed in the Islamic scriptures;
It has the sanction of all the four ages.
Meat is the attraction of festive occasions
     and weddings
Where a great deal of meat-eating is done.
Man and woman are born out of flesh.
So are sovereigns and sultans.
If you find them going to hell,
Why must you accept their charity?
It is strange justice;
The one who gives goes to hell

And the recipient is destined for heaven!
O Pandit! You don't seem to understand yourself
And yet you instruct others.
What type of a guide are you?
O Pandit! You know not where flesh originates.
What are corn, sugar-cane and cotton
      produced from?
From water the three worlds are created.
"I have several uses," says the water,
"I have many forms, too."
"Why must one give up such dainties
And become a recluse?"
Says Nanak, after serious thought.

(1289-90)

Slok I

The splendour of the world is transitory;
My perverted mind doesn't remember the grave.
I am mean, lowest of the low.
My Lord! You are like the river.
Grant me only one favour.
Everything else is poison which I crave not.
With the skill of Your craftsmanship
You have instilled life in the fragile pot
      of my body.
Because of Your potential, I've gained power.
Nanak is the frenzied dog of Your Court;
His frenzy dwindles every day.
The world burns like a bonfire,
Only God's Name exudes comfort and peace.

(1291)

Raga Prabhati

Prabhati I

By the grace of the Guru one gains knowledge,
By reading and understanding one gains glory.
One is enlightened within
And is endowed with the nectar of His Name.
God! You alone are my spiritual guide;
I ask You one favour:
Bless me with Your Name.
I have disciplined five volatile intruders.
My self-conceit is gone.
My dirty looks and perverted thinking
*   have vanished;*
Such is Your Divine message!
Bless me with the rice of chastity and continency
And the wheat of compassion
And the leafy plate of corn.
Endow me with the milk of Your mercy
And the clarified butter of patience.
I ask for all this in utter humility and
*   spirit of charity.*
Forgiveness and patience are my milch-cow
And poise the calf that drinks its milk.

*My garments should be the Lord's praise and
    modesty
And thus should Nanak continue to
    remember You.*

(1329)

Glossary

Arati. Hindu ceremonial for propitiating the deity.

Atharva Veda. One of the Hindu philosophical works.

Azrael. The messenger of death.

Bani. Sikh scriptures; spoken from the mouth of the Guru.

Barah Mah. Twelve months; a poetic form describing every month of the calendar. It is usually the pangs of separation of the beloved from her lover. In Sikh scriptures, it is the soul separated from the Divine Entity.

Bhakti. Loving devotion to God.

Brahma. Hindu god of creation.

Devi. Hindu goddess.

Dharamraja. Hindu god of justice.

Dharamsala. A place of worship. Also a rest-house for travellers.

Dharam Khand. The realm of righteousness.

Dhaval. The mythical bull believed to be supporting the earth.

Bhakta. Devotee.

Durga. A Hindu goddess.

Dwaparyuga. Age of penance.

Eight Miraculous Powers. Anima (Adopting another's form), Mahma (Expanding one's body), Laghima (Reducing one's body) Garima (Enhancing one's weight), Prapti (Acquiring whatever one desires) Prakamya (Guessing what is in someone's mind), Ishta (Persuading others as one desires) Vashta (Taking everyone under one's control).

Guru bani. The holy words uttered by the Guru.

Havan. A Hindu ceremonial.

Holy Granth. The Sikh Scriptures.

Indra. Hindu god of rain and thunder.

Ishwar. The Creator God.

Janeau. Sacred thread worn at the time of what may be called Hindu baptism.

Japu. Repetition of the Name of God.

Jnan Khand. The realm of knowledge.

Kaliyuga. Age of fire.

Karam Khand. The realm of grace.

Karma. The deeds one does which one has to account for.

Khatri. A Hindu caste (Kshatriya).

Krishna. A popular Hindu god.

Madhusudan. Vishnu who annihilated Madhu.

Madrasa. A teaching outfit associated with Islamic studies.

Manji. A place where the devotees foregather.

Mulla. The Muslim priest.

Nine Doors. Nine physical senses like audio, visual, etc.

Nine treasures. In the shastras they are named after precious stones in Gurbani these are joy in God, poise, enlightenment etc.

Parvati. Consort of Shiva.

Patwari. Land record keeper.

Puranas. Hindu sacred tales and legends.

Qazi, Magistrate. Also written as Qadi.

Qur'an. The sacred text of Islamic scriptures.

Rabab. A string musical instrument more popular in the north-west of the Indian sub-continent. Guru Nanak is said to have improved upon it by introducing silken strings.

Sach Khand. The realm of truth.

Sadhukari. A link language popularised by saint-poets in Northern India.

Samadhi. A shrine over the ashes of the dead; deep meditation.

Saram Khand. The realm of activity.

Satyayuga. Age of truth.

Sat Kartar. God is truth.

Shastras. Hindu sacred writings.

Shikari. A hunter.

Shiva. Hindu god of destruction.

Siddha. An ascetic.

Sidh Gosht. A long composition in which Guru Nanak has recorded his dialogue with the ascetics of his time.

Six Schools of Philosophy. Believed to be the path to salvation.

Slok. Couplet or short stanza.

Smritis. Hindu sacred writings as remembered.

Sohila. A poetic form; eulogy, also bed-time prayer of the Sikhs.

Sufi. A mystic cult associated with Muslim seekers.

Tantric. An adherent of Tantra, an esoteric doctrine regarding rituals.

Tenth Door. Supreme spiritual realisation.

Three states of mind. These are: Satva (peace), Rajas (passion) and Tamas (ignorance, darkness).

The Vedas. Ancient Hindu scriptures. There are four Vedas.

Tretayuga. Age of continenace.

Udasi. A sect of Hindu seekers who have renounced the world.

Vaid. Physician.

Vaishnav. Followers of the Hindu god, Vishnu.

Var. Ode, a poetic form in which usually the exploits of the legendary heroes are sung.

Vishnu. Hindu god of preservation.

Word. Message; text of the hymn.